Library of
Davidson College

The First World Disarmament Conference 1932–1933

AND WHY IT FAILED

Other Titles of Interest

HALL, R. L.
Black Separatism and Social Reality

LASZLO, E.
The Inner Limits of Mankind: Heretical Reflections on Today's Values, Culture and Politics

PECCEI, A.
The Human Quality

HALL, B. L. & KIDD, J. R.
Adult Learning for Development

TOWNSEND COLES, E. K.
Adult Education in Developing Countries, 2nd Edition

ECKHOLM, E.
Losing Ground: Environmental Stress and World Food Prospects

EPSTEIN, T. S. & JACKSON, D.
The Feasibility of Fertility Planning

TICKELL, C.
Climatic Change and World Affairs

LEBEDEV, N. I. M.
A New Stage in International Relations

SHANKS, M.
European Social Policy, Today and Tomorrow

The First World Disarmament Conference 1932–1933

AND WHY IT FAILED

by

PHILIP NOEL-BAKER

Honorary Fellow, King's College, Cambridge, Personal Assistant to the President of the Disarmament Conference, 1932, Minister of State, Foreign Office, 1945, Secretary of State for Air, 1947, Secretary of State for Commonwealth Relations, 1948, Nobel Peace Prize, 1959.

PERGAMON PRESS

OXFORD . NEW YORK . TORONTO . SYDNEY . PARIS . FRANKFURT

U.K.	Pergamon Press Ltd., Headington Hill Hall, Oxford OX3 0BW, England
U.S.A.	Pergamon Press Inc., Maxwell House, Fairview Park, Elmsford, New York 10523, U.S.A.
CANADA	Pergamon of Canada, Suite 104, 150 Consumers Road, Willowdale, Ontario M2 J1P9, Canada
AUSTRALIA	Pergamon Press (Aust.) Pty. Ltd., P.O.Box 544, Potts Point, N.S.W. 2011, Australia
FRANCE	Pergamon Press SARL, 24 rue des Ecoles, 75240 Paris, Cedex 05, France
FEDERAL REPUBLIC OF GERMANY	Pergamon Press GmbH, 6242 Kronberg-Taunus, Pferdstrasse 1, Federal Republic of Germany

First edition 1979

British Library Cataloguing in Publication Data
Noel-Baker, Philip, *Baron Noel-Baker*
The first world disarmament conference, 1932–1933.
1. World Disarmament Conference, 1932
I. Title

327'.174'0924   JX1974   78-40922

ISBN 0-08-023365-1

Reproduced, printed and bound in Great Britain by
Cox & Wyman Ltd, London, Fakenham and Reading

TO

The survivors of Hiroshima who have spent so many hours of public conference and private conversation in describing to me the devastation and terror of the day the first atomic bomb fell on their city, and in telling of their shattered lives since then, with grievous physical mutilations and deformities, and without the families and friends whom they judged to have been more fortunate than themselves, because the bomb had killed them.

"I confess that I cannot go all the way with your view that war is necessarily evil in itself. History records many just wars of aggression . . . . . Whatever you do, war will come sooner or later, and if you carry Disarmament too far and crush the military spirit, your civilization will go under. Decline of civilization is connected with the decline of military spirit".

Sir Maurice Hankey to Lord Cecil, August 18th, 1925.

Contents

Contents

Acknowledgements

This book has taken me a long time to prepare. I owe a debt of gratitude for help, encouragement and suggestions to far more people than I have space to name. They will, I hope, remember what they did for me, and accept these words as an expression of my appreciation and my thanks.

I must, however, pay a special tribute to some of them.

My life-long friend, Monsieur Louis Dolivet of Paris, did outstanding work for the League of Nations before 1939, when he was very young—work which earned him the confidence and admiration of many leading men, including Lord (Robert) Cecil and Monsieur Leon Blum, then Prime Minister of France. He has maintained his interest in the United Nations and the cause of world disarmament. He has most generously financed the research which this book required, and has helped me to get it published. Without his encouragement and support, the book would have been abandoned long ago.

Mrs. Helen Gahagan Douglas, with whom I had the privilege of working in the General Assembly of the United Nations, has likewise persuaded me that I must go on, at times when I was inclined to give up.

Miss Lorna Lloyd of the University of Keele, and Mr. Dan Smith, of the Richardson Institute, have helped me greatly in research.

The Very Reverend H. C. A. Gaunt of Winchester, and Dr. David Holloway of the University of Edinburgh, have read the manuscripts, and have saved me from falling into error on many points.

Miss Helen Armstrong has helped me very much, as she did when I wrote an earlier book, *The Arms Race*.

My friend, Mr. David Bar-Kar, has done much to facilitate and accelerate the final preparation of the text.

I have received invaluable assistance and most useful suggestions, from two well-qualified students of international affairs, Miss Alison Williams and Miss Lois Galza.

In the last stages of my work Miss Pauline Court has helped me with great generosity and great ability.

I record my warmest thanks to them all.

Finally, I must record my special debt of gratitude to Mr. John Edwards. By a happy chance, I made Mr. Edwards' acquaintance, and received his almost full-time help, during the last weeks of my work on this book. I cannot overstate what I owe to his kindness, his industry, and his encyclopaedic knowledge on everything to do with armaments, disarmament and war. He is already an established authority on these subjects, and his writings will do much to improve the chance of final victory for reason and for common sense. I offer him my heartfelt thanks.

April 10th, 1978   PHILIP NOEL-BAKER

President John Fitzgerald Kennedy

The starting-point and final goal of this book were stated on September 26th, 1961, in a speech to the United Nation's General Assembly by President John Fitzgerald Kennedy:

"For we far prefer world law in the age of self-determination, to world war, in the age of mass extermination.

"Today, every inhabitant of this planet must contemplate the day when it may no longer be habitable. Every man, woman and child lives under a nuclear sword of Damocles, hanging by the slenderest of threads, capable of being cut at any moment by accident, miscalculation or madness. The weapons of war must be abolished before they abolish us.

"Men no longer debate whether armaments are a symptom or cause of tension. The mere existence of modern weapons—ten million times more destructive than anything the world has ever known, and only minutes away from any target on earth—is a source of horror, of discord and distrust. Men no longer maintain that disarmament must await the settlement of all disputes—for disarmament must be a part of any permanent settlement. And men no longer pretend that the quest for disarmament is a sign of weakness—for in a spiralling arms race, a nation's security may well be shrinking even as its arms increase.

"For 15 years this organisation has sought the reduction and destruction of arms. Now that goal is no longer a dream—it is a practical matter of life or death. The risks inherent in disarmament pale in comparison to risks inherent in an unlimited arms race".

President Dwight D. Eisenhower

(Commander-in-Chief of the Allied Forces for Invasion of Normandy on 'D' Day June 4th, 1944) White House Press Conference, 1957.

"I know of nothing that has occurred in our time where greater optimism must be maintained . . . . . than in this whole business of getting disarmament . . . . . The alternative is so terrible that you can merely say this: all the risks you take in trying to advance are as nothing compared to doing nothing, to sitting on your hands".

Preface

For some years I have been engaged in writing a book which is intended to bring the argument for world disarmament and the de-militarization of the world society of states up to date.

As part of this book, I included an outline history of negotiations for Disarmament from the Hague Conference of 1899 from the Rescript by which Czar Nicholas II summoned the First Hague Conference in 1898 to the convocation of the Special Session of the United Nations General Assembly devoted to Disarmament in 1978.

When this work was nearly complete my friend, Miss Helen Armstrong, suggested that the historical chapters would be of more interest, if I added autobiographical reminiscences about proposals, episodes and Conferences of which I have had personal experience; and if this history were put at the beginning of the book.

This seemed to be most valuable advice. For the purpose of the historical outline is to show that international Disarmament negotiations have not failed because of any inherent technical difficulty in drawing up the necessary Treaty; they have failed because men in positions of authority or influence have wanted them to fail, and have striven successfully to make them do so.

It was logical, as Miss Armstrong suggested, that this should come at the beginning of the book, and that it should be followed by the study of the present arms race, and of the dangers which have resulted from the failure of the earlier efforts to disarm.

When this large work was almost ready for the printer, Monsieur Louis Dolivet proposed that the chapters dealing with the World Disarmament Conference of 1932 should be made into a shorter study and published before the meeting of the Special Session of the General Assembly of the United Nations devoted to Disarmament.

As the Special Session is only the second World Conference ever summoned to deal with the problem of competitive national armaments, and the danger of war to which this competition leads, it may be useful to

remind the Delegations, the Press and the public of what happened at
the first.

I hope it may serve to warn those who are striving to make World
Disarmament succeed, of the activities of those who hope that it will not.

The reader may find a repetition of certain points in more places
than one—I ask his forgiveness if this is weariness; I hope the repetitious
way serve to leave the points more finally in his mind.

Introduction

Behind us lie
The thousand and the thousand and the thousand years,
Vexed and terrible.
And still we use
The cures that never cure.

Christopher Fry, *A Sleep of Prisoners*

What happened to disarmament?

Disarmament, on which great hopes were built, and for which leading statesmen[1] worked and staked their reputations and their careers throughout this century?

What happened to the League of Nations and the United Nations, which were the only beneficent result of the sacrifice made by many millions of young soldiers who were killed in two World Wars?

It is the purpose of this book to face these questions, and to find an answer.

On August 19th, 1918, twelve weeks before the First World War ended, Robert Cecil wrote the following letter to Sir William Wiseman, for transmission to President Woodrow Wilson of the United States:

"Here we are", said Cecil, "suffering from the greatest catastrophe that has, perhaps, ever occurred; and the worst part of it is that it seems to herald an era of destruction"
(prophetic vision!). . . . . . .

"What is wanted is a great ideal, and that must be found in the Hebrew . . . . and Christian, conception of the reign of peace . . . . We must give it an organ of expression. That must be . . . . a League of Nations."

1   See footnote on p. 3 below.

1

Cecil then went on:

> "I am not sure that he [the President] realized the immense difficulties there will be in the way of establishing a League of Nations. All the European bureaucracies will be against the idea, including probably the bureaucracy of this country. Nor must it be forgotten that the heresies of militarism have unfortunately extended beyond the limits of Germany, and all the militarists will be against the idea. . . . All these people are working already, more or less secretly, against the idea. . . . . .

> "If I venture to insist upon the strength of the bureaucracies in Europe, it is because no-one who has not actually seen them at work can form any idea of their resisting power. They are very able and honourable, but they are past masters of the art of obstruction and resistance."[1]

Three months before the First World War ended, while the carnage was still going on, so close across the English Channel—from his Sussex garden Robert Cecil could hear the never-ceasing thunder of the guns; in his imagination, by day and night, he heard the screams of the dying and the mutilated men—*three months before the carnage ended, the bureaucrats and militarists were already working against a League to keep the peace.*

Four decades later, Dwight D. Eisenhower, a victorious General and a President of the United States, warned his compatriots, and other nations, against the influence of what he called "the military-industrial complexes" of the world.

For all that time the struggle which Cecil had foreseen was going on. It is still going on in 1978.

It is a struggle—national and international, within national Governments and Parliaments, and in the international Conferences and Institutions—between two groups of men, equally 'honourable' and patriotic, but sharply, even passionately, divided in their views.

On the one hand are the men who believe, with Eisenhower, that:

> "War in our time has become an anachronism which can serve no useful purpose"[2]

1 Lord Cecil of Chelwood, *All the Way*, 1941, pp. 142-144.
2 President Eisenhower, Address to U.S. Society of Newspaper Editors, April 21st, 1956.

and who, therefore, believe that "disarmament is a continuing imperative" (Eisenhower) and who work for lasting peace, world disarmament
and the rule of law in international affairs.

On the other hand are the men who believe that to hope for lasting
peace is to indulge an idle dream, that "there will always be wars", and
that therefore the Government of every nation must be left free to
maintain whatever armaments they consider they require.

The bureaucrats and militarists hold their views with all the sincerity, indeed, with all the moral fervour, of the "internationalists" whom
they oppose. Politicians, diplomats, general staff, officers, arms manufacturers, military correspondents and commentators in the Press, the
radio and television, they believe that they alone understand the true
interests of their nations. Their *motives* must command respect.

On November 30th, 1918, 3 weeks *after* the Armistice, I came back
to London from the Front to join the League of Nations Section of the
British Foreign Office. In our first conversation, Cecil, who was my
Chief, read me the letter to Sir William Wiseman which I have quoted.
Fresh from 4 years of War, I found it almost impossible to believe that
anyone could be against a League to keep the peace.

My eyes were shortly opened. The very first document laid on my
table in the Foreign Office was a famous minute by Sir Eyre Crowe, a
senior civil servant, who was soon promoted to be the head of the British
diplomatic service. Crowe sought to prove that a world disarmament
treaty would be technically impossible to make. It was only a first
attempt to convert me to a 'realistic' view.

There will be many readers who feel as I did on November 30th,
1918. Unpersuaded by the joint authority of Robert Cecil and Dwight
Eisenhower, they will say:

"No, all that can't be true. *Everybody* wants disarmament, lasting
peace, and the rule of law. But, alas, experience has shown, in all
these Conferences and Commissions, that Crowe was right: a Disarmament Treaty *is* technically impossible to make; and without
Disarmament, the rest, of course, has failed."

With all respect, this is the exact opposite of the truth. The Conferences and Commissions have proved that all the technical problems of
Disarmament *have* been solved; that the further Disarmament were
taken, the more swiftly and completely would the difficulties disappear.

The only problem that remains unsolved is that of creating the popular support that will enable—or compel—the statesmen to see it through.

The Conferences and Commissions have proved something else: that there *are* men, very powerful men, in the delegations and in their Governments at home, who do *not* want Disarmament, and the rule of law; men who hate and fear them, and who fight against them with all the tenacity and skill of which Cecil wrote to William Wiseman. For many years after November 1917, I was personally involved in the struggle; I knew the men and what they did.

In that struggle for three-quarters of a century, the internationalists have won all the arguments, but the bureaucrats and militarists have won all the material victories that count.

They sterilized the First and Second Hague Conferences in 1899 and 1907. The Conferences were summoned by Czar Nicholas II and by President Theodore Roosevelt to end the arms race; but the arms race was never seriously discussed.

They finally destroyed the Hague Conference Movement altogether; the Third Conference was planned, the date was settled, but it never met.

In 1919 and 1920 and 1924, they opposed and defeated the obligatory jurisdiction of the Permanent Court of International Justice—the very kernel of the policy of the rule of law.

They destroyed the League of Nations Conference on Disarmament in 1932–3, after President Hoover of the United States had made proposals on which the Conference came very near to full success.

With encouragement from British, French and other militarists, the German armament manufacturers brought Hitler into power.[3] Without their massive purchase of the German Press, Radio and Films, and without their financing of his SA and SS private armies, Hitler would have remained an unknown and unimportant Munich clown.

In spite of its remarkable successes, they destroyed the League of Nations.[4]

They have destroyed the binding force of the United Nations Char-

---

3   Most notably Krupp, Hugenberg and Thysson. See Philip Noel Baker, *The Private Manufacture of Armament*, Chapter 7.

4   See Chapters 12 and 13, below.

ter Law; they have taken us far back along the road to the international anarchy of pre-League days.

The motives of these bureaucrats and militarists were 'honourable' and, according to their lights, patriotic. But their guilt, before history, and before past, present and future generations, is appalling.

The human race has paid a fearful price for their triumphs.

The waste, suffering and horror of the two World Wars were beyond description, with ten million killed in the First, and fifty-three million in the Second.

The terrors of the third, for which the militarists are so busily preparing, challenge the imagination of every thinking man.

The world expenditure on armaments in 1978, *at constant prices*, was almost eighteen times the world expenditure of 1913, before the Kaiser's war. It has increased since then.

This unproductive expenditure on preparation for war—all the millions since 1945—has been a major cause of the galloping inflation, of the famines in many hungry lands, and of the general economic and financial chaos which threatens a breakdown of industrial civilization.

These are the true results of the victories won by the bureaucrats and militarists since the Czar summoned the First Disarmament Conference in 1899.

Yet always they have called themselves the 'realists'; they have claimed that they "faced the facts of an imperfect world".

In truth, they have always been the prophets of illusion. They have preached the ancient Roman fallacy: *Si vis pacem. Para bellum*—"more armaments will prevent war". They said that before 1914, before 1939, since 1945; and they say it still today.

In truth, it has been the internationalists who have been the realists, the men who really faced the facts, the men whose policy would have averted the wars and the disasters that have followed in their train.

It was Liddell Hart, the most eminent of all military historians and students of strategy, who wrote that, if the Disarmament Conference of 1932 had been allowed to make the Treaty of Qualitative Disarmament which it had prepared,[5] the aggressions of the Dictators in 1939 and 1940 would have been impossible;[6] and therefore no Second World War.

5 Deterrent or Defence, p. 250, 1960.
6 op. cit. p. 254

It was Sir Winston Churchill who said that the Second World War should be called the "Unnecessary War", that it "could easily have been prevented if the League of Nations had been used with courage and loyalty by the associated nations."[7]

In 1978 the true realists are still the men who stand for the United Nations, world disarmament and the rule of law. Only their policy can avert the cataclysm with which the following chapters deal.

More than ever before, the bureaucrats and militarists are, in 1978, the prophets of illusion—and of doom.

Yet today they seem to be in charge of policy, more perhaps than ever before.

But, however terrible the defeats the internationalists have suffered in the past, however deep the dogmatic slumber in which the peoples are at present sunk, Robert Cecil's struggle for world disarmament and the rule of law is not yet over.

The United Nations still exists.

The obligations of its Charter, won by the blood and sweat and tears of two World Wars, are still the law which is professedly accepted by the Governments of the Members of the UN.

It is fitting to remember, in the daunting and disorienting days of 1978, the iron nerve and steadfast faith of Robert Cecil.

Cecil was the true creator of the League of Nations. In 1941, when his life-work lay in ruins, with war in every continent, and Hitler's bombs falling around his London and his Sussex homes, he wrote the book about the League from which his letter to Sir William Wiseman has been taken.

On the title page of the copy which he gave me, he wrote the words:
"Le jour viendra"
The day will come.

7 Cecil, *All the Way*, p. 224.

CHAPTER 1

The Unended Struggle:
Hawks versus Doves

What happened to Disarmament?

The question is not even asked, still less answered, by most of the professional historians and by others who write about the twentieth century.

Yet the question, and the answer, are the key to any proper understanding of what has happened to individual nations, and to the human race, since this century began.

The question and the answer are the key to the most dramatic sequence of events, to periods of radiant hope, and to the direst tragedies, that imagination could conceive.

They are the key to the crisis of the 1970s—military, economic, political. In finding the answer, and in acting on it, lies the hope for the survival of mankind.

Pledges, Principles and Plans

What happened to Disarmament?

What happened to the First Hague Conference, summoned in 1899 by Czar Nicholas II of Russia, and to the Second, summoned in 1907 by President Theodore Roosevelt of the United States? Both conferences were assembled with the same high purpose in view—to end the arms race and to establish lasting peace. What happened to them in the end of all?

What happened to Article 8 of the Covenant of the League of Nations; to Part V of the Treaty of Versailles; to Article 26 of the Charter of the UN? All three were solemn, binding, legal obligations, by which the Governments promised world disarmament. What happened to them when the League and the UN began their work?

What happened to the plans for drastic world disarmament drawn up in 1932 by President Hoover of the United States? By J. Paul-Boncour, Prime Minister of France? And in March 1933 by Stanley Baldwin, Prime Minister of Britain?[1]

What happened to the Six Principles on which Disarmament negotiations should be based, drawn up by President Truman in 1952, and endorsed by the UN General Assembly in September of that year?

To the Eisenhower–Kruschev Resolution of 1959, calling for General and Complete Disarmament, jointly sponsored by *all* the 82 Members of the UN?

To the McCloy–Zorin principles of 1961, on which world Disarmament should be founded, likewise unanimously endorsed by the General Assembly?

To the Draft Treaties of General and Complete Disarmament submitted by President John Kennedy and Chairman Kruschev to the UN Committee of Eighteen in 1962?

What happened to all these pledges and proposals? They were put forward by a Czar of all the Russias, by Presidents and Prime Ministers of the most powerful military nations.

They were enthusiastically welcomed by the vast majority of the other states.

What happened to them?

They did not fail, as some 'experts' would maintain, because the technical difficulties of a Disarmament Treaty could not be solved; as said above in the Introduction, the technical difficulties of disarmament have all been solved.

The Hawks

They failed because the process of securing political agreement on a Treaty was long and complex; because the process was far longer and more complex than it should have been; because the men who sought to make a Treaty, the internationalists, allowed themselves to be obstructed and delayed by other men in powerful positions who thought

1   For an account of these plans, see Chapters 7–12 below.

that lasting peace and world disarmament were an idle and a dangerous dream.

Throughout the century, in almost every country, there have always been such men; men who were immoveably convinced that future wars were sure to come; who felt their nations must be free to fight these wars with unfettered hands; to whom, in consequence, Covenants and Charters and Kellogg Pacts were 'scraps of paper'; men who felt with passion that it was their patriotic duty to work against, and to defeat, as they did defeat, the Hague Conference Movement, the Disarmament Conference of 1932, the League of Nations over Abyssinia, and the Disarmament proposals made since 1945 in the UN.

Some readers will reject that statement with a sense of outraged disbelief. "No", they will say, "it simply *can't* be true. *No-one* would work against the League or Disarmament or the UN."

But it *is* true; and it is the answer to the question with which this chapter began. That is the lesson of my whole experience, which started with the Hague Conference of 1907, and of which I shall say more before this chapter ends.

Sir Anthony Nutting

It is the lesson of Sir Anthony Nutting's political career—the brilliant young Minister of State in the British Foreign Office, who ended his career by resignation in 1956. He resigned because the hawks had induced the Western Governments in 1955 to do a *volte face* on the Anglo-French Memorandum—the proposal for a First Stage Treaty of Disarmament prepared by Selwyn Lloyd and Jules Moch.

Nutting had played a major part in persuading Moscow to accept the Memorandum, and its withdrawal was to him a bitter blow. Worse was to follow; not long after, under the influence of the hawks, the French and British Governments launched the charter-breaking Suez War. It was too much, Nutting resigned. It was a serious loss. He would have been an outstanding international leader, of the kind whom Britain and the UN have so gravely lacked.

In a restrained account of the events in which he was involved, Nutting wrote:

"The student of this melancholy piece of history must always bear in mind—as the negotiators for their part were never allowed to forget—that behind each disarmament delegation there hovers that gaunt grey giant in the affairs of men and nations, the Ministry of Defence."[3]

In other words, the hawks.

Professor Bernard Feld

The same lesson emerges from the experience of Dr. Bernard Feld of the United States.

Dr. Feld is an important witness. As a young graduate student, he was chosen by Dr. Leo Szilard to help in the very first experiments that were made to find out what chance there might be of developing an atomic bomb. Dr. Feld worked for many years in U.S. Military Research; he was in close and constant touch with various Governments. He has been Secretary General of the Pugwash Movement; he is now Professor of Physics at the Massachusetts Institute of Technology, and Editor of the *Bulletin of the Atomic Scientists*.

Writing in 1975, almost 20 years after Nutting, Dr. Feld said as follows:

"There is a universal tendency among intellectuals to think of the world as divided into peace-loving and aggressive nations—although we differ as to which nations fit into which classification—and that the problem of ensuring peace is one of getting the aggressive nations to behave like the peace-loving ones; that the achievement of peace depends primarily on the process of negotiation between sovereign states. My experiences over the last 15 years, involving a wide variety of international intercourse, have convinced me that this is a dangerous delusion. In every country of which I have any firsthand knowledge, and this covers nations governed by all systems and all ideologies, there are people whose basic orientation is peaceful and people who firmly believe in the need for and efficacy of force: people who—in much over-simplified terminology and for want of a better categorization—can be referred to as doves or as hawks.

3 *Disarmament*, 1959. Preface.

"*I am firmly convinced that the achievement of peace and international order depends more on the outcomes of the continuing hawk-dove struggles in each country than it does on the confrontations between their leaders.* I have accumulated enough evidence to convince me that—tacitly and without establishing any formal cabal—*the military hawks of the world have learned how to work in concert, how to reinforce each other and to divide the opposition*, so as to convert every international arrangement as well as each international crisis into an internal victory for their hard-line approach.

"We doves, on the other hand, remain divided by conflicting ideologies and by our acceptance of a false dichotomy between national and ideological loyalty and loyalty to mankind. But the threat we all face can only be conquered if we learn how to overcome our inessential, (*inessential*), differences and if each of us—united in a common program for achieving a safe, peaceful and livable world—pursues these goals in our own country in such a way as to strengthen each other's effectiveness.

"The survival of mankind demands a new approach which, with all due respect, might adopt as its new slogan: 'Doves of the world, unite; you have nothing to lose but your planet'."[4]

---

4   "The Charade of Piecemeal Arms Limitation", *Bulletin of the Atomic Scientists*, January 1975.

The Work of the Hawks:
Detailed Autobiographical Evidence

The judgements just quoted from Sir Anthony Nutting and Professor Bernard Feld are couched in general terms. So is the personal conclusion that I stated on pages 4–5 above—though I have said that it is based on a long experience of inter-Governmental disarmament negotiations and debates.

"Couched in general terms"—but there is a mass of detailed evidence available to support these judgements.

In earlier works, I have published much of it: *The Geneva Protocol*, 1925; *Disarmament*, 1926; *The Coolidge Conference*, 1927; *The Private Manufacture of Armaments*, 1936 and 1972[5]; *The Arms Race*, 1958 and 1960.

There is further evidence in the following pages.

But, nevertheless, it may be useful, if I begin this book by giving an autobiographical account of some of the episodes in my life which have convinced me that the hawks have been, and are still—indeed are now more than ever—the enemies of mankind; and that there is no issue of national or international policy that compares in importance with that of ending war and dismantling the war machines that devour so great a part of mankind's annual dividend of wealth, and which keep so many nations in a paroxysm of suspicion, conflict and fear.

---

5   There were two editions in 1936; the second was a Left Book Club Paperback, Dover Publications, New York, republished it with an up-to-date Introduction in 1972.

CHAPTER 2

Sir Maurice Hankey, Secretary of the Cabinet 1919–1939

Hankey, though he never held any Ministerial office, played a most important part in forming British foreign policy between the wars.

Hankey was a man of quick understanding and great ability. Before the war of 1914, he had been Deputy Secretary of the Cabinet Committee of Imperial Defence, under his outstanding chief, Lord Esher. Hankey had had a large hand in drawing up what was called the Cabinet's War Book—the detailed planning of the action that must be taken by every Department and every organ of Government when the war began.

When the war was over, Parliament voted him a sum of £25,000 in recognition of the service he had rendered in promoting victory. He was appointed to the new and very influential office of Secretary of the Cabinet. This gave him daily personal access to the Prime Minister, and instant access to any other Cabinet Minister whom he desired to see. In this capacity, he won the confidence and trust of almost every Prime Minister and Foreign Secretary from the Armistice in 1918 onwards for many years—they included Lloyd George, Stanley Baldwin, Ramsay MacDonald, Curzon, Austen Chamberlain, and others. Cecil had such admiration for Hankey's gifts that he asked him if he would accept the office of Secretary General of the League. Hankey fortunately refused, and later, when Hankey published what would have been his plan for the organization of the League Secretariat, Cecil agreed that we had had a fortunate escape.

I had a good many contacts, and some strange experiences, with Hankey during the many years while I was a Temporary Civil Servant or a Parliamentary Private Secretary in the Foreign Office. Two of them were so significant, and gave me such an insight into Hankey's character and thinking that I must recount them at length.

One late afternoon in March or April, when I was firmly established as head of Cecil's League of Nations Section of the British Delegation to the Peace Conference in Paris, and when, as it happened, I was head-over-ears in urgent section work, I received a sudden summons from Hankey to appear at his Cabinet Office in London at 11 a.m. the next day. As there was then no night service across the Channel, and as aircraft were only just beginning to make the journey,[1] Hankey had arranged that I should have a fast limousine to drive me through the night from Paris to Boulogne, where at dawn I would board one of His Majesty's Royal Navy destroyers. The destroyer would deliver me to Dover, where another fast car would meet me, and deliver me to Hankey's office at 11 a.m.

It was an exhausting, but on the Channel, a fascinating trip. The stretch from Paris to Boulogne was sheer hell. The French had not repaired the road since the war. It was full of potholes, and of what seemed like gaping chasms, all the way. My unhappy driver suffered greatly, trying to steer around the hazards and yet to make good time—I knew the feeling well; the roads at the front, pock-marked with shell-holes, were even worse, and there we had only been allowed the tiniest of lights.

But at least my driver had the compensation, or so I hoped; of double overtime. For my part, I bounced and rolled in the back of the car for 6 or 7 hours, trying in vain to sleep, to find a tolerable position in which to sit, cursing freely, wondering what grave national emergency had imposed this hideous trial on me.

There are times when I hate motor-cars with a deadly hatred, and this was one of them.

The destroyer, by contrast, was a sheer delight. I was the only passenger, the ship had come from Portsmouth to pick me up; the officers were hospitable and charming; nothing was too much trouble for them.

After a good breakfast while we were still at anchor, we left Boulogne harbour and found a very stormy sea. I was normally very sea-sick; I expected 4 hours of misery and shame. In fact, the movement

---

1   I did cross by air a few weeks later, and remarkably unpleasant it turned out to be.

of the destroyer was so exciting, and the waves so beautiful, that I stood on deck in keen enjoyment all the way to Dover.

The drive to London was much better than the drive from Paris the night before. But still I could not sleep, and my weariness and resentment were intense.

Why had my evening's work been so incontinently interrupted? Why had this ghastly inconvenience been imposed on me? What justified the waste of public money, the destroyer's special voyage, the chauffeur-driven cars?

I got the answer the moment I reached Hankey's office. There was no reason, no excuse, at all for all this discomfort and waste of public money and of my time. I could just as well have finished my work and come by train and Channel steamer, and seen Hankey at 6 o'clock that evening instead of 11 a.m., or even at 11 a.m. the next day. Hankey only wanted to offer me a new and different job. He proposed that I should leave Lord Robert Cecil, and join the staff of the Prime Minister, Lloyd George.

He tried to make it sound extremely urgent. If I said "yes", I must return at once to Paris, come back again tomorrow, and start in No. 10 the following day. It sounded hollow; in the nature of the case, there was no real urgency at all.

He tried to wrap it up in glamour. I should have to be a personal assistant to Lloyd George, with access to him whenever I desired. I should have to work with the House of Commons—and I wanted some day to be a Member? I should have to go back to Paris when Lloyd George returned. I should have, with my wife, to spend the summer at Le Touquet (I think it was Le Touquet) with Lloyd George and his family on their holiday.

I was simply furious. The journey, the urgency, the destroyer and the cars, had been a fake—a fake designed to impress me—to make me feel the excitement and the *power* of the world which I should enter if I said "yes".

What if all the glamour was a fake as well? It occurred to me to doubt—and in 1978 I doubt it even more—whether Lloyd George himself had ever heard of this proposal. Some years later I knew well people who had worked in No. 10 during the year or two that followed the World War; I came to know Lloyd George, and even stayed with him at Churt. No-one ever mentioned this urgent, glamorous offer that I should work for him, or the fact that I refused.

For, of course, without a moment's hesitation, I refused. After 4 months in his service, I was deeply devoted to Lord Robert. I had seen him in the League Commission leading, persuading, opposing, convincing Prime Ministers and Foreign Secretaries; I thought him the greatest of men. I was passionate about the League, and profoundly conscious that with Lord Robert I should have the chance to help in shaping it—Lord Robert always listened gladly to my suggestions, and sometimes they reached the Covenant; and, later on, I might have the chance to help to make a living League of Nations work. Not for a single instant did I hesitate; I *could* not throw this most glorious chance away. And I knew that my father would have thought that I was right.

Hankey, when he understood my blank refusal of his offer, was at first astonished, and then angry, angry beyond control. He snapped out vicious things about my lack of foresight, my stupidity, the future on which I was going to turn my back. Then he said snide things about Lord Robert, and made me even angrier than I had been before.

Then, only wanting to wound me, he talked contemptuously about the League. "I could have been the Secretary General, if I'd wanted to", he said with hot disdain. I had known about Lord Robert's offer, but it shocked me greatly that he should blurt it out to me. I broke off our conversation as abruptly as I could; left his office with a feeling of discomfort and disgust; went to see my mother, who told me I'd been right; and then took the next train back to Paris, arriving there that night.

I had learnt that Hankey was a hawk; that he was an active enemy of the League; that I must treat him with caution and suspicion if our paths should cross again. And I had the feeling, perhaps quite foolish, but persistent, that his real purpose was not so much to get me to join the Prime Minister, Lloyd George; it was rather a Hankey plan to break up my partnership with Lord Robert, and to divert a young fanatic from his labours from the League.

I have told this story of my first personal confrontation with Sir Maurice Hankey in great detail, partly because it is the detail that is revealing about his thinking, his methods, and his character; partly because, as I said before, he was to exercise great influence on British Government policy about the League.

The story of my second personal confrontation with him was even more fantastic; it will seem to many readers even more improbable, than the first.

After April, 1919, we met fairly often, in Paris, in his office in London, in the Treasury building, sometimes, if I had to go there, in No. 10. But our contacts were nearly always brief and insubstantial; only rarely did I have to talk about some point that really mattered. Always we were both self-conscious, if not embarrassed; always both remembering that unhappy and unnecessary episode in April, 1919.

It was ten years later, in August, 1929, that we had to work together for a longer time.

It was at an Anglo-French-German Conference in Holland, at which two burning questions were discussed and settled—the distribution of reparations that the German Weimar Republic were paying still to Britain and France; and the possible evacuation from the Rhineland of the French and British Forces which, in pursuance of the Treaty of Versailles, had occupied it since that Treaty came into force.

The British delegates were Philip Snowden, Chancellor of the Exchequer, and Arthur Henderson, Foreign Secretary in MacDonald's Second Labour Government, which had come to office 3 months before—once again, unhappy Labour, in a minority in the House of Commons.

Snowden had brought with him my friend, Sir Otto Niemeyer, of the Treasury, and his Treasury Private Secretary, P. J. Grigg, whom Winston Churchill made Secretary of State for War in 1940 or 1941. Henderson had brought Sir Cecil Hurst, Nigel Ronald, one of his Foreign Office Private Secretaries, and me—I had been elected member of Parliament for Coventry in the General Election, and Henderson had made me his Parliamentary Private Secretary.

We were housed in the best hotel in Scheveningen, the seaside suburb of The Hague. It was a most agreeable hostelry, with excellent facilities for swimming in the sea, which I did every day; and with a marvellous dance band, which pleased me even more! I danced *every* evening with a charming damsel, Niemeyer's lady secretary—a wonderful secretary, as I discovered; a wonderful performer on the dance-floor; and a delightful person, who later married a distinguished Civil Servant, the head of a great Government Department.

The French delegates were Briand, Foreign Minister in a French Government of the Centre-Left; the Minister of Finance, a Norman whose name I cannot recall; they had with them Rene Massigli, who for more than 10 years always attended the Council and the Assembly of the League as the top official from the Quai d'Orsay. Of course, I knew Massigli extremely well, and was glad to welcome him when he came to London as de Gaulle's Ambassador to Britain in 1942—his escape from Vichy France was an adventure. Massigli was an able man, but I always found him, as did Sacha Grumbach and others of his French colleagues, more diplomatic than League-minded men like me.

The German delegates were two Social Democrats, Party Comrades, and Stresemann, the Foreign Minister, already very ill.

It had been agreed beforehand that Snowden should be President of the Conference, and that Hankey should be Secretary General; Hankey would organize the Conference, control the Secretariat, arrange the meetings, propose procedure and the rest.

Snowden had small experience of international work; Hankey not so very much more, although he had a reputation as a clever fixer. Henderson, who *had* experience of international work, watched them in silence with amused interest or concern.

Snowden was guided in everything by Hankey, and Hankey proceeded to put into practice his own pet theory of how things should be done. This meant that the Conference should not meet in Plenary Session all the time; it should meet to do formal business: to express gratitude to the Dutch, to settle the Agenda—then, as required, to register approval of agreements which Hankey had secured by private conversations with the various delegates one by one.

This had several inconveniences, of which one was the fact that important Ministers would sit around in their hotels with nothing much to do. I felt some sympathy for Hankey's plan when, after several days, a Plenary was held for a general discussion of the Reparations problem, and of how the German money should be shared by Britain and France.

The discussion in this Plenary meeting had not gone very far when Snowden started the most violent international quarrel I had ever seen.

In all British innocence, Snowden told the French Minister of Finance that the argument he had used was "grotesque and ridiculous".

"Grotesque and ridiculous", in English, was quite in keeping with the kind of gentle *badinage* that Snowden exchanged with Winston Churchill in the House of Commons every day. But in French, and in an international meeting, it was devastating, deadly, personally and publicly insulting to the Frenchman in the highest possible degree. The Minister of Finance was not a Norman for nothing. In a manner worthy of William the Conqueror, he replied to the attack. I wondered how the Conference would get back to serious work again; for days the fatal words, "grotesque and ridiculous", went on reverberating through the Delegations' meetings and hotels, and through the columns of the Press.

In the end, Snowden himself was hoisted with his own petard. He argued, and bullied, the Conference into agreeing that Britain should receive a larger proportion of the reparations which Germany would pay. But the increase in Britain's share was to be delayed for many years. Britain's share, so the final Agreement laid down, would become larger in the 1960s and 1970s. This was hailed as a British triumph. But, under the impact of the world slump which was just beginning in August, 1929, German Reparations were finally abolished by a Conference in Lausanne in July, 1932. Snowden's triumph then looked, as indeed it was, "grotesque and ridiculous", and his participation in the Hague Conference, and Hankey's help to him, not so very significant in the long history of man.

But my second long confrontation with Hankey happened earlier in the Conference. After Hankey had spent 2 or 3 long days in his private consultations with the various delegates one by one, he came back to the hotel one evening at 10 p.m., utterly exhausted, as it seemed, in body and mind. I happened to be standing in the hotel entrance as he came in. I think he wanted someone on whom he could vent his spent-up exasperation—his day had not gone well.

"Come and talk to me while I have some supper", he said at once. I was reluctant; I wanted to go and dance; but there had been some carefully suppressed tension between Henderson and Snowden,[2] and I thought it right to agree.

Hankey ordered supper, and an expensive bottle of champagne. He invited me to share it, but I thanked him and refused, and he drank it all.

He began by talking about his day; about the French and German delegates, about Reparations and the knotty problems the Conference had to solve. Then, as the champagne did its work, he turned to Geneva and the League and Cecil (who had resigned from the Tory Government in 1927). I remember nothing specific he said about these subjects, nothing like his contemptuous outburst 10 years before. But he left me with the same feeling of discomfort, the same conviction that he was hostile to it all. As he finished eating, and drank the last glass of his champagne, he began to talk more quickly. He wasn't drunk. I am sure Hankey was never drunk in all his life. But his inhibitions were relaxed, and he went on talking in a different and more aggressive strain. This part I repeated the next morning to Arthur Henderson, to Cecil Hurst, to my young Treasury dancing friend; I have talked about it constantly since then to Robert Cecil and to many more; although, till now, I have never written it down, I am very certain that I remember clearly what he said.

"You know, Noel-Baker", he began, "you think you're right, but you're really quite wrong about it all. If you could make things happen as you want them to, you would take out everything that's most worthwhile, everything that's great and noble from the life of nations and of men."

"Noble" sounds a bit too pompous for his informal, but excited dinner table talk; but I am sure that he said "noble", and I think he said "beautiful" as well. "You would rob us of what is greatest, noblest, most beautiful, in the past, present, and in times to come. The world would be a drab and dreary place, with your League of Nations, if you had your way."

He did not say in words: "war is the true test of greatness, both in

2 The tension in fact, was about *me*, Grigg had perceived that I was on friendly terms with Briand and Massigli; he told Snowden and Hankey that I was traitorously caballing with the French, and undermining Snowden's stand. It was a pure invention; Massigli complained that I was most unfriendly, because I would not lunch with him. But Snowden listened to Grigg's invention, and sent Henderson a formal complaint about me.

nations and in men. If you ended war, you would deprive the nations of what moves them to their best and finest efforts; you would take away the glory that calls forth the magnificent response of young men who volunteer to sacrifice their lives. You would wipe out the splendid thrill, the excitement, the adventure that a regiment of soldiers feel, as they go to fight for the honour and the interest of their people at home. Nations and individuals would stagnate; they would soon become lethargic, spiritless; they would lose all inspiration; the effect would be disastrous, in science, in industry, literature and even art. You would eliminate the hope of victory in war, that is, of the grandest achievement of which any men can dream. If I had had no war experience, my life would have been empty, barren, almost worthless to me. If I saw no chance of any war ahead, I should have nothing to stir my mind or my imagination, no task that would make it seem worthwhile to work, to plan—to be alive."

The words I have put in quotation marks above are not, of course, what Hankey actually said. They are my interpretation of what he wanted me to understand.

He never actually used the key word 'war'. But we both knew exactly what he meant. He was well aware that Henderson and I spent a large part of every day in talking about the League and how it could be made to work, and about Disarmament. I understood him to be telling me, as plainly as he dared to, that he was implacably against us, that he would oppose us tooth and nail.

I remember that I went to bed more certainly convinced than ever that Hankey was a resolute and most industrious hawk.

This view has been confirmed in 1978 by what Hankey wrote about the League and Disarmament in 1925—not long after he had played a major part in destroying Cecil's T.M.A., and after he had persuaded Stanley Baldwin, Austen Chamberlain and other Ministers to kill the Geneva Protocol. The following are extracts from documents he wrote in 1925, now to be found in the British Public Records Office:

1. A letter from Sir Maurice Hankey to Sir Cecil Hurst.*

---

* Dated 22 Jan 1925 Hankey played a major part in securing the rejection by Britain of Cecil's Treaty of Mutual Assistance in 1924, and of the Geneva Protocol in 1925. These episodes will be described in my larger book: "Third Time Dead: Armaments Civilization", to be published in 1979.

"I have read your paper on Sanctions, with considerable interest. As a matter of fact, it does not alter my conception of the functions of the League. Personally, I dislike sanctions, and I believe that the first time the League tries to use them against any Great Power, it will come a cropper. They may occasionally bluff or bully a small state, but the moment they try it on with a big state, the greater number of Members will refuse to express any opinion, and the remainder will divide into two camps."[3]

As the purpose of sanctions was to restrain and, if necessary, to defeat aggressive war, Hankey's use of the word "dislike" is highly significant. Hankey did not *want* to restrain or to defeat aggressive wars by the use of collective international strength.

2. This is made even plainer by words he wrote to Cecil on August 18th, 1925:

"I confess that I cannot go all the way with your view that war is necessarily evil in itself. History records many just wars of aggression."[4]

3. Hankey sought to mitigate the unfavourable impression which his letter might make on Cecil by adding the following sentences:

"My argument, then, is not for war, but for caution lest we bring down civilization with a crash. I don't agree that public spirit is a substitute for military spirit. The military spirit is necessary even in the League, if it is to carry out the Covenant. It is certainly necessary for the British Empire."

Cecil would not be likely to agree that ending war would "bring civilization down with a crash", and in 1978 it is clear that ending war has become the only way to preserve civilization. Already in 1925 wiser, and greater, men than Hankey had understood that this was so. Lord Grey of Falloden had written: "The nations must disarm or perish."

4. But Hankey's view of armaments and war was unbridgeably remote from that of Grey and Cecil.

As said, above, he rejected their condemnation of war as "necessarily evil in itself".

5. Still more important, he thought that war would be *inevitable* in the future, as he thought it had been inevitable in the past.

"Whatever you do", he wrote in his letter to Cecil of August 18, 1925,

3 Cab. 63/37.
4 Cab. 63/39. Letter from Hankey to Cecil.

"*War will come sooner or later,* and if you carry Disarmament too far, and crush the military spirit, your civilization will go under. . . . Decline of civilization is connected with decline of military spirit."

6. He explained this more explicitly in a Memorandum which he sent to Cecil, and which he had the temerity—some would say, since he was addressing Cecil, the impertinence—to entitle "Introduction to the Study of Disarmament". There were 15½ pages of it, in double-spaced stencil; but the essence of the argument is set out in the following phrases:

"It would be easy to lull the nations into a false sense of security, each relying on a support from its neighbours which may not be forthcoming when the crisis comes. It would be easy in a long period of peace to dull the consciousness of nationality in which alone the military spirit can survive. The symptoms of degeneracy manifest themselves so gradually that in any given moment they are not easy to discern. . . . . He who goes wisely, goes slow."

What Hankey says about "sanctions" and "security" in this passage, and in the letter to Hurst which was quoted above, was of supreme importance in determining the course of history between the Wars. His words were in the nature of a self-fulfilling prophecy; they expressed what he *hoped* would happen, and what, in so far as he influenced British policy, he was able to *make* happen. Since his influence on British policy was great at the moments of crisis*, and since British action was decisive in undermining and destroying the League, and so causing the Second World War to happen, his burden of responsibility is great indeed.

7. But even more important for the present purpose are the words he wrote about War, which have been quoted above. War is not "necessarily an evil in itself". This challenges the whole purpose of the League.

And then the fundamental proposition on which, then and still now, militarist philosophy is based:

"Whatever you do, war will come sooner of later."

It is *inevitable* that there will be wars in future. Since war is the supreme test of a nation, and victory is its supreme interest, *nothing* can matter so much as strong armaments and a virile military spirit. Viewed against this background of the certainty of war, Covenants and Kellogg

* See p. 21 N.

Pacts are scraps of paper; military strength must be the guiding principle of international policy.

If Hankey's thought is followed to its logical conclusion, wars are not only inevitable; they are desirable, and even necessary. We must hope that they will happen at regular, and not too infrequent, intervals. For in "a long period of peace . . . degeneracy" will set in and "civilization will perish."

This is the true interpretation of the thinking that guided Hankey and many other powerful British hawks between the Wars.

It was more prevalent, more crudely expressed, and more brutally applied by the hawks (Nazi and non-Nazi) of Germany, by the Comté des Forges and other hawks in France, by the militarists of Japan and other lands. But the fundamental propositions on which *their* thinking was based did not greatly differ from those of Hankey and other British Hawks.

Between the Wars I thought it catastrophic that a man holding such views should for 20 years have the power to exercise great influence on British policy. I still think it so today.

Of course Hankey was not alone. In the decisive years of the 1930s, when the fate of the League was decided and most promising proposals for disarmament destroyed, he had the help of many others—Ministers and officials alike. Principal among them were Sir Warren Fisher, Head of the Treasury and the Civil Service, and Sir Robert Vansittart, Permament Under Secretary of State for Foreign Affairs.

Vansittart's biographer, Ian Colvin, wrote the following words: "Sir Samuel Hoare, (then for a brief period Foreign Secretary) found the pertinacious Sir Warren Fisher, head of Treasury, critical of the Foreign Office organization;" but equally he remembers him as "wholeheartedly engaged with Vansittart as his chief colleague in preparing plans for intensifying British rearmament".[5]

My concern is to make the reader understand that there are still many men who share these views, and who hold positions of great influence in their Government administrations in 1978.

But I should do Hankey an injustice, if I said nothing more of his qualities of mind and character.

He was a very clever, and a very hard-working public servant. He

5   *Vansittart in Office* by Ian Colvin, pp. 63–64.

was truly patriotic, very proud of being British, *wholly* dedicated to what he thought to be the interests of the British people, the British Government, and the Empire which they ruled.

His biographer sums up the eulogies he had made of him in the following words:

"Hankey was a patriot and an Imperialist . . . . Hankey believed with passion that the British Commonwealth and Empire in whose cause he worked throughout his life, though like all human institutions they had their faults, were as a whole a very powerful influence for peace and for the well-being of many millions of people . . . . If he, in common with many others, misread the diabolical phenomenon that was Hitler, he did at least recognise as early as 1932 that the time had come when there was no alternative to rearmament. On matters of judgment, whether it be the development of the Tank and the aeroplane to break the deadlock on the western front in 1915 or the need to win the Atlantic Battle rather than devastate German cities in 1942, or the dire consequences which would stem from insistence on Unconditional Surrender in 1943–45 this biographer finds it extremely hard to fault him."*

This seems to me a just and admirably fair assessment of Hankey as a leading figure in British public life, and in the formation of British foreign policy between the Wars.

But there are two points in Mr. Roskill's tribute to Hankey which seem to me to bear out everything that I have written in this chapter.

Hankey, says Mr. Roskill "misread" the phenomenon of Hitler, "but recognised already in 1932 that there was then no alternative to re-armament".

This is to say, in terms, that when Hankey was faced in 1932 by the question that the Foreign Secretary, Sir John Simon, put to the Cabinet and to the House of Commons, "Shall we accept world disarmament, or shall we allow Germany to re-arm?", Hankey, faced with this fateful option, deliberately chose to allow Germany to re-arm, knowing that it would be Hitler who re-armed her; knowing that this was to ensure a frenzied arms race, and an arms race that would end in war.

To say this is not hindsight. It was foreseen in 1932 that if the Disarmament Conference was allowed to fail, there would be a frenzied

* Stephen Wentworth Raskill: "Hankey, Man of Secrets", Collins 3 Vols, 1970 to 1974.

arms race, that Hitler would re-arm Germany, and that it would end in war. This was foreseen, and *foretold*, by Cecil, Henderson, Lloyd George and many others. Hankey "in common with many others" (i.e. in common with the appeasers, the bureaucrats and the militarists) was catastrophically wrong.

For there *was* an alternative to re-armament in 1932, as the following chapters of this book will prove. That alternative remained open even as late as 1936. Mussolini's aggression in Abyssinia could have been defeated then by the League of Nations, and it would have been defeated by British leadership.

Mr. Roskill sweeps the League aside with unrestrained contempt—contempt which, no doubt, reflects the contempt felt for the League and all its works by Hankey himself—contempt which Hankey made me feel so vividly in all our personal contacts.

But there were others among his contemporaries, besides Cecil and Henderson and Lloyd George, who did not share Hankey's contempt for the League of Nations.

In 1944, when the Second World War was almost won, Sir Winston Churchill wrote to Cecil words which will be quoted again in later chapters:

"This war could easily have been prevented, if the League of Nations had been used with courage and loyalty by the associated nations" (meaning Britain and France).

"Easily" is Sir Winston's word. His authority on these events seems to me of greater weight than Mr. Roskill's.

I do not dispute that Hankey deserved the recognition and reward that Parliament gave him for the service he had rendered before and during the First World War. It was a fitting climax to his life-long service to Conservatism, as he understood it, when he was made a member of the House of Lords in 1939.

But the quotations from his writings which I have made above, are of over-riding significance. I reinforce them with one more quotation. Stephen Roskill records that Hankey's thesis was as follows:

"If Disarmament is carried too far and too fast, a decrease in national virility would result. Unemployment would be created and trade would suffer, also that the ideals for which the League of Nations stood were already out of date."

This sad homily of mingled economic fallacy and chauvinist pre-judice only shows that Hankey failed to understand the Covenant, or the general policy and thinking of the statesmen who drew it up. That reinforces my absolute conviction, formed from my own experience many years ago, and now confirmed by my study of the records of the past, that Hankey, personally, and as a man who influenced history, was actively and always a dedicated hawk.

CHAPTER 3

The Coolidge Conference, 1927:
U.S. and British Hawks

The opponents of the Geneva Protocol argued that it would drive the United States still further from the League; that it would once more be a fatal obstacle to the entry of the United States into Membership.

In fact, the Fifth Assembly, by demonstrating the will of the great majority of the Members of the League to outlaw all war for good and all, and to achieve World Disarmament at an early date, did very much to change United States' opinion about the League and to end or mitigate the indifference or hostility which so many Americans had felt.

So much so, that when President Coolidge decided in 1927 to summon another Naval Conference to supplement the work done in Washington in 1922, he felt able to summon it to meet in the League building in Geneva, and to arrange that the Secretary General and his staff should act as the Secretariat of the Conference. This was a remarkable change in the attitude of the U.S. Government, but U.S. public opinion seemed cordially to approve.

Unfortunately, the Conference was a failure, thanks to mistakes of procedure, and to the work of hawks both in Britain and the United States.

The Washington Conference had been convoked to end a race in the construction of battleships and aircraft-carriers between the United States, Britain and Japan. It had succeeded in effecting a large measure of naval disarmament—a large reduction in the number of capital ships and aircraft-carriers of the three Powers.

In 1927 a new naval race was beginning in the construction of cruisers. Coolidge thought this dangerous; he wanted to stop it, and to effect reductions in the numbers and tonnage of all the remaining categories of "auxiliary" warships; (i) cruisers; (ii) destroyers and torpedo-boats; and (iii) submarines.

When the Conference met in the League capital in June, 1927, Coolidge's delegate, Hugh Gibson, the U.S. Ambassador to Belgium, laid an ambitious plan before his British and Japanese colleagues—France and Italy had decided not to accept his invitation. The plan would have meant a large reduction of numbers of ships and total tonnage in each category for all three Powers. Coolidge proposed that the ratio should be that adopted in the Washington Treaty, 5:5:3.

The crucial points in this proposal were two:

First, a reduction in cruisers which would have cut the numbers in the British Fleet from over 70 to 50, with a total cruiser tonnage of 400,000 tons;

Second, 'parity' (i.e. equality of naval strength) between the U.S. and the British Fleets in each category of ships.

This was a reasonable, and highly desirable, next step in naval disarmament, which would have ended the danger then in sight, and helped to prepare the way for a World Disarmament Conference which the League was expected to summon rather soon.

The two British delegates to the Conference were both members of Baldwin's Cabinet, Mr. Bridgeman, M.P., First Lord of the Admiralty, and Lord Cecil. They *both* wanted to accept the Coolidge Plan; they both considered that it would be safe and wise for Britain to do so. But they had had no advance information about what the plan would be; their first knowledge of it was when they heard Hugh Gibson read it out in the opening Plenary (and public) session of the Conference. Cecil told me, when the Conference was over, that he thought this a sad mistake on the U.S. president's part.

What made matters worse, and much more difficult for Bridgeman and Cecil was that they, too, had brought a plan which they had been instructed to lay before the Conference, and of which their British Government had given Coolidge no prior notice or information. Cecil likewise deeply regretted this failure to consult Washington in advance, for which he was himself in no way to blame.

This British plan was what the Admiralty were pleased to call a proposal for naval disarmament—but a proposal much less dovelike than the plan which Hugh Gibson had read out.

There were three important, and controversial, points in the British Admiralty's plan:

First, they proposed to extend by 6 years the 'life' of the capital ships which the three Powers had retained under the Washington Treaty; this would save, they said, a large sum of money on new construction during these 6 years;

Second, that when these capital ships were in due course replaced, their maximum displacement tonnage should be reduced from the 35,000 tons allowed by the Washington Treaty to 30,000—this, they said, would save £1 million per vessel:

Third, that cruisers should be divided into two subclasses:

(i) vessels of not more than 10,000 tons displacement, armed with 8 inch guns;

(ii) vessels of 6,000 tons displacement, armed with 6 inch guns.

Bridgeman explained that the "offensive" power of a 10,000 ton 8-inch gun cruiser was 2½ times as great as that of a 6000 6-inch gun vessel; that this second sub-class could be called "defensive weapons", while the former sub-class was offensive; that the British Admiralty wanted more of the 6000 ton 6-inch gun cruisers to deal with commerce raiders. These smaller cruisers, said Bridgeman, would cost £500,000 less to construct than the 8-inch gun vessels.

These proposals seemed to the British Admiralty to constitute 'disarmament', because they would reduce the cost of the naval budgets of the three Powers.

But Hugh Gibson had as his principal naval adviser Admiral Jones, of the U.S. Navy, who was by no means a dove, and who shared what was then in the U.S. Navy a common suspicion of the British.

He found the British proposals unacceptable.

Under the Washington Treaty, Britain had been allowed to keep some large capital ships (e.g. the armoured cruiser, *Hood*, 41,000 tons) which gave her a larger total tonnage than the U.S. and Japan. Admiral Jones did not think it consistent with parity that this advantage should be retained for an extra 6 years.

Second, the U.S. Navy wanted to be free to build as many 10,000 8-inch gun cruisers as it wanted to, within the total cruiser tonnage limitation of 400,000 tons. The 10,000 ton vessels had a much greater cruising range than 6000 ton vessels; this did not matter to the British, because they had naval bases all around the world. But the U.S. Navy had very few bases; they could not allow themselves to be handicapped as the British proposed.

These were serious divergences of view. They were exacerbated by another eminent British naval personality who was at the Conference.

Admiral-of-the-Fleet, Lord Jellicoe, Commander-in-Chief of the British Fleet at the Battle of Jutland in 1916, had been sent by New Zealand to the Conference as their delegate. He explained with passion the "absolute requirement" of the British Admiralty of 70 cruisers to protect our shipping time of war.

Britain, he said, depended on her ocean-going merchant ships for raw materials and food. If the ships stopped coming for 6 weeks, we should starve and our factories would close down. We had started the war in 1914 with 114 cruisers—they had not been enough; the German submarines had sunk hundreds of thousands of tons of British merchant ships. The 'Trade Routes' we must patrol and police totalled 80,000 miles—70 cruisers was the minimum number we required.[1]

A brilliant British naval writer lost no time in analysing, and ridiculing, Jellicoe's strategic doctrine. Commander Stephen King-Hall, M.P., had fought under Jellicoe in a battleship at Jutland. He had since become a Member of Parliament and a foremost broadcaster for the BBC. Jellicoe's theory of an "absolute requirement", he argued, was absurd. The number of cruisers we required for commerce protection depended on the number of enemy cruisers which could act as commerce raiders. If all cruisers were abolished by all the Naval Powers, Britain, which had the largest Merchant Fleet, with the biggest and fastest ships, could at once dominate every trade route and every sea. We should mount 6-inch guns on the fastest ocean liners; these vessels could destroy all submarines or other vessels that could attack our merchantmen.[2]

Hugh Gibson likewise challenged the doctrine of an "absolute requirement" in the Conference. But Bridgeman and Jellicoe refused to give it up, and stuck to their figure of 70 cruisers.

Gibson's Admiral Jones was all too ready to think that the British, with their plan to keep *H.M.S. Hood* and other large battleships for an extra 6 years, and their demand for 70 cruisers, were trying to go back on

1 See Toynbee, *Survey of International Affairs*, 1927, p. 59.
2 See Philip Noel-Baker, *The Coolidge Conference*, 1927.

parity between the British and the U.S. Fleets. Bridgeman and Cecil called on Gibson to accept their assurances that this was not so.[3]

But Admiral Jones was not reassured. He was a hawk, and he called in a hawk's jackal, an American professional (some would say prostituted) propagandist, William Shearer, who lobbied against Disarmament for the U.S. naval shipbuilding firms. These firms had paid Shearer £5000 to come to Geneva to work for 6 weeks; he was to 'post' the Press on why the Coolidge Plan was dangerous to the U.S.A., and to work for the failure of the Conference in every way he could.

My friend, Mr. Arthur Sweetser, sent me a firsthand account of Shearer's campaign, and of how the American Admirals had used him.[4]

"Yes", said one of the Admirals, "we know that bird. He is coming in mighty handy for us at the moment. We are making use of him. If necessary, we will spike his guns when the time comes."

The U.S. Admirals told their Press men to go to Shearer for information, and Shearer gave them prepared articles, and 'background' memoranda, full of false or distorted figures and arguments, and all very strongly anti-British in tone.

This was bad behaviour by the U.S. Admirals, for Shearer was a well-known character, with a disgraceful record in Washington and elsewhere.

He had had a contract earlier with the well-known "isolationist" or chauvinist newspaper proprietor, Mr. William Randolph Hearst. Hearst had paid Shearer £400 a month to write against the League and the Permanent Court of International Justice.[5]

Shearer boasted in a letter, written in January, 1928, to the head of the Bethlehem Shipbuilding Company, Mr. Wakeman, who had employed him to go to Geneva, that:

3   Toynbee, *Survey of International Affairs*, p. 51.
4   The text of Mr. Sweetser's letter to me can be found in *The Private Manufacture of Armaments*, p. 361. I was unable to use his name when that book was published, as he was the leading U.S. member of the League Secretariat. In his letter, Mr. Sweetser said, *inter alia*: "The American delegation was dominated by the Navy Board at Washington.... These men [U.S. Admirals in Geneva] like their opposite numbers in the British delegation, argued all technical, and, many political questions on the assumption that war was inevitable between the United States and Great Britain." Mr. Sweetser lived to render great services to the United Nations, as he had done to the League. He died, too young some years ago.
5   Philip Noel-Baker, *The Private Manufacture of Armaments*, p. 3.

"As the result of my activities during the Sixty-Ninth Congress, eight 10,000-ton cruisers are now under construction."[6]

Shearer's proceedings in Geneva, like those in Washington and elsewhere in the U.S.A., were an utter disgrace. It throws a sad light on the morals of the U.S. naval shipbuilders that they employed him; it is a convincing illustration of what the Covenant called the "evil effects" of The Private Manufacture of Arms.

But it was not Shearer who made the Coolidge Conference fail. He stirred up bad feeling between the United States and British Navies, and to some extent he roused anti-British feeling in the U.S.A.

But the distinction of causing the Conference to fail went to none other than Winston Spencer Churchill, who in 1927 was Chancellor of the Exchequer in the British Government.

Briefed by Admiralty hawks, and no doubt remembering his days of glory when, in 1914, he was First Lord of the Admiralty, and mobilized the British Fleet for the beginning of the First World War, Churchill opposed what he called "mathematical parity", between the British and the U.S. Fleets.[7] He succeeded in winning the Cabinet to his side. They summoned Bridgeman and Cecil to return to London; in their pressure decided that Britain must not accept "mathematical parity" with the U.S., and that the British delegates must resist the U.S. demand that they must be free to put 8-inch guns on all their cruisers.

Cecil thought this last U.S. demand was wrong; but he was sure that the U.S. would insist on it, and he thought it "madness" to allow the Conference to fail on such a point. He therefore warned the Cabinet, that, if the Conference broke down, he would resign.[8]

The Conference did break down, and Cecil did resign. The day after he came home, he gave me a full account of all that he had suffered in his 6 weeks in Geneva in the Coolidge Conference.

In plain English, Churchill's ploy about "mathematical parity" meant that he wanted Britain to be free to have a larger fleet than the United States. In 1978 that looks as grotesque an absurdity as Cecil thought it in 1927.

6 Ibid.
7 Churchill made a public speech to this effect on August 6th, 1927. Toynbee, *Survey of International Affairs*, p. 74.
8 Toynbee, *Survey of International Affairs*, pp. 63–65.

But Cecil cared about Disarmament, and the stable peace which Disarmament would bring. The hawks, British and American, did not care about Disarmament, and most of *them* thought stable peace an idle dream.

It is only by recalling that, that we can understand what happened in the Coolidge Conference.

But one other reflection must be added.

Two weeks after the Conference failed, during the Eighth Assembly, the Secretary General of the League, Sir Eric Drummond, whose Personal Assistant I had been for several years, made me a considerable discourse on what had happened. Drummond had come to the Secretariat from the British Foreign Office; he had been a firm believer in the value of *secret* (or non-public) diplomacy. Experience in the Council and Assembly of the League had gradually converted him to Cecil's principle—"Publicity" (i.e. public debate) "is the life-blood of the League."

On September 1st, 1927, Drummond said to me:

"The mistake was to do the work in private sessions. If the Conference had been held in public, it could not have failed."

If Drummond was right—and I found no-one in Geneva who disagreed—it meant that the hawks could not have done in public what they did in private, and that the public in Britain, the U.S.A. and elsewhere would have insisted, if they had known what was happening, that the Conference should succeed; they valued Disarmament more, and understood it better, than their Governments.

This is a lesson which, with Eric Drummond's authority, should be remembered when the Special Session of the UN General Assembly meets to discuss Disarmament in 1978.

CHAPTER 4

Sir Robert Vansittart, Permanent Under-Secretary of State for Foreign Affairs

The sequel to the Coolidge Conference was not what Winston Churchill and his colleagues had expected.

They had made a bold gesture for the Royal Navy. They had allowed an International Conference, summoned in Geneva by the President of the United States, to end in failure and confusion. The cause of the failure was the British refusal to agree to what the United States desired. They confidently believed that the British people would rally behind the Royal Navy, and endorse what they had done.

But they had miscalculated. The revulsion against the First World War was still extremely strong—and against "the old diplomacy" which had allowed the war to happen. Foreign policy was fast becoming the most important theme in British politics, with the support for the League of Nations the concrete issue on which electors made up their minds.

Already before the Coolidge Conference met in June, 1927, the League of Nations Union had begun a vigorous campaign for the basic policies of the Compulsory Arbitration of International disputes and World Disarmament.

The Union had found public opinion very receptive on both these major issues. The audiences at their public meetings—the meetings happened by the score almost every night—listened gladly to speakers who urged the drastic international reduction of all armaments and the establishment in world affairs of the rule of law. The editors of local papers printed the letters of leading members of Union branches. Branches were very ready to send deputations to their MPs. The Labour and Liberal Parties kept these issues constantly before both Houses of

Parliament, and the issues were given large coverage in the national Press.

Thus it happened that, when the Coolidge Conference broke up, and Cecil resigned, general British opinion swung heavily to his side.

The Labour Party were quick to exploit this favourable circumstance. After the War the National Executive of the Party had appointed an Advisory Committee on Foreign Affairs, of which Leonard Woolf (the eminent husband of Virginia Woolf) was the Secretary. Other members of the Committee included G. Lewes Dickenson, Norman Angell, J. A. Hobson, H. N. Brailsford, Charles Roden Buxten and—thanks to Arthur Henderson—myself.

When a General Election came in sight in 1929, the National Executive invited Leonard Woolf and me to draft the large section of the Party's Election Manifesto which dealt with foreign policy. We were given all the space we wanted; our draft, which we called "The Seven Pillars of Peace", took up nearly half the final document. It was accepted by the National Executive without the change of a comma, and it was very favourably received by the Press.

Naturally, support for the League, Disarmament and Compulsory Arbitration was the theme of "The Seven Pillars".

Simultaneously, the League of Nations Union issued an Election Questionnaire to the candidates of all Parties, in which the candidates of all Parties were invited to state their views on these issues. The candidates' answers were always published, compared and analysed in the local Press.

Union branches in more than 600 constituencies held meetings at which all the candidates were invited to speak and to answer questions.

These meetings, with audiences which included numerous supporters of all three Parties, were nearly everywhere the best of the campaign. In the famous city of Coventry, where I was running for Labour—my second of twelve Parliamentary Elections—we had a packed hall, a vocal audience, endless questions, and a joyous time.

In these meetings, as in their answers to the LNU Questionnaire, Labour candidates were naturally guided by "The Seven Pillars of Peace".

As the result of all this, and, above all, as the result of Cecil's resignation from their Government, the Tories lost heavily in the General Election in May, 1929. Labour came back to the House of Commons as the largest Party, with 289 seats; the Tories had 245, and the Liberals, under Lloyd George, had 58. This meant that a second Labour Government came to power, far stronger than the first—but still a minority government who could be turned out by the Liberals at any moment.

When MacDonald formed his Cabinet, his first inclination was to take the Foreign Office himself, as he had done in 1923. His second was to choose J. H. Thomas, the leader—the very popular and successful leader of the National Union of Railwaymen. But Arthur Henderson was strongly of the view that *he*, and not Thomas, should be Foreign Secretary. He felt that his experience as President of the Labour and Socialist International, and his success with the Geneva Protocol in the Fifth Assembly of the League, made it both his right and his duty to claim the Foreign Office. MacDonald resisted for a little while, but Henderson's position in the Labour Party, his high standing in the country, and his influence abroad, made his claim irresistible.

On the day he was appointed Secretary of State, Henderson asked me to be his Parliamentary Private Secretary. This was an unpaid office, but half-a-century ago it carried privileges that have now been abolished. On Foreign Office matters in the House of Commons, I was expected to speak and vote in favour of Government policy; on all other matters I was free to speak and vote as I desired. (When, in fact, I voted against the Government on Unemployment Benefit, MacDonald called me in and lectured me; I defended myself by saying that a generation earlier my father had often voted against *his* Government. Henderson said no word of disapproval of my vote, with which, I think, he secretly agreed.)

For the rest, I had a table in the Private Secretaries' Room in the Foreign Office; I saw all the telegrams, in and out, exchanged with embassies abroad; I saw any paper diverted to me by the Principal Private Secretary, Walford Selby, before it went in to the Secretary of State, and both Selby and Henderson invited me to write any minute on them that I thought it useful or worthwhile to write. And Henderson told me, on my first day in the office, that he would want me to travel with him wherever he went, and that he would make me a delegate to the Assembly of the League. This proved to be an advantageous plan for all concerned. I knew the ropes in Geneva better than most; I knew the

Secretary General, Drummond, and the whole Secretariat, very well; and I had friends, friends, in almost every delegation.

In the Office I very soon became real friends with Walford Selby. Walford had been Principal Private Secretary to *four* Secretaries of State—Arthur Balfour, Curzon, MacDonald, Austen Chamberlain—Arthur Henderson was his fifth. He was a man of shrewd judgement, and great generosity of character, of whom I still think with the warmest admiration and affection.

Selby very quickly understood Henderson's great qualities. He would walk across the room, with slow, careful steps, in imitation of Henderson's measured tread: "Master won't be bounced into any follies", he used to say.

Something happened rather soon that brought us close together. When Henderson took office, the Permanent Under-Secretary of State, the Civil Service head of the British Diplomatic Corps, was a certain Ronald Lindsay, not a brilliant or effervescent man, but solid, dependable and *loyal*.

Lindsay, like Selby, had thoroughly approved what Henderson had done in his first week in the Foreign Office. Henderson had asked Selby to summon to a meeting in his room the heads of all the different departments of the Office. When they had all gathered in his room, Henderson addressed them somewhat as follows: "Gentlemen, you are serving a new Government, and they have a new foreign policy. We laid this policy before the Electorate in our Manifesto; the electorate approved it, and, with your help, we are going to carry it out. Here it is." And Henderson read them the "Seven Pillars of Peace".

"We shall need your help", he ended, "I count on it, and I know we shall have it."

Lindsay, speaking for all his senior colleagues, told Henderson that he would have their help; and he meant it.

But rather soon—in July or August, if I remember rightly—there came a bombshell from No. 10. Lindsay was due for promotion to a post abroad and he was nominated by Henderson to become Ambassador to the United States of America. But his successor in the Foreign Office was not appointed by Henderson as might have seemed normal Government practice.

During the Lloyd George regime after the war, Sir Austen Chamberlain as Chancellor of the Exchequor had signed a minute, approved by the Cabinet, under which senior appointments in Whitehall were to be made by the Head of the Treasury, who also became the Head of the Civil Service. This gave the Head of the Treasury a wide power of patronage among his colleagues of the Civil Service in Government Departments.

When Sir Austen Chamberlain became Foreign Secretary in 1924, he rejected an interpretation of this minute which would have meant that the then Head of the Treasury, Sir Warren Fisher, could have appointed the Permanent Under Secretary of State for Foreign Affairs. But in 1929, when Lindsay went to Washington, Sir Warren Fisher unearthed the minute of 1919 and insisted that it gave him the power to appoint whosoever he chose to take Lindsay's place.

In pursuance of this claim, he appointed Robert Vansittart, who for 5 years had been Private Secretary to the Prime Minister in No. 10.[1]

The true significance of this appointment lay in the fact that Sir Warren Fisher was an ardent advocate of the increase of British armaments and that Vansittart took the same view. Indeed it can be said that Vansittart's intellectual equipment for the office of Permanent Under Secretary of State consisted of three ideas alone:

He had a bitter hatred for, and distrust of, Germans.

He believed that war would surely come again and that British armaments of all kinds should be increased to the maximum extent that the Treasury could be persuaded to allow.

He hoped with ardour that Italy (meaning Mussolini) would be our ally in the next war when it came.[2]

This appointment was clearly unwelcome to Walford Selby, and I guessed that it would be unwelcome to others in the Office. There were a number of men who were senior to Vansittart who was only 49 years of age; and I thought then—and still think—that these other men were not

1 The facts of this strange proceeding are to be found in a book *Diplomatic Twighlight* by Sir Walford Selby, Preface, pp. iii–iv.
2 Vansittart's biographer, Ian Colvin, records that in his first conversations with his new Foreign Secretary, Sir Samuel (Hoarde) in 1935. Vansittart said that one of the "stark facts" (of the international situation) was that "it was essential to Britain to have a friendly Italy in the Mediterranean", *Vansittart in Office* by Ian Colvin, pp. 66–67.

only senior to but also abler than Vansittart. Vansittart was being promoted over their heads.

I remember Selby saying to me, "This is Hankey's doing" I had a firm conviction from the first moment I heard of the appointment that it *was* 'Hankey's doing". I discussed it often at the time with people who were in a position to know, and I have always remained convinced that it was so.

In any case, the appointment was Sir Warren Fisher's and everybody in the Foreign Office knew, that Hankey was a close ally of Sir Warren Fisher.

And, in any case, the appointment was not Henderson's, although Vansittart was to be Henderson's principal adviser, not only on other appointments, but on every issue of the policy Henderson was to pursue. I remember Henderson relapsing into heavy silence when I talked about Vansittart's advent to the Office.

It was not pleasing to Selby or to me that the appointment should be "Hankey's doing".

I had my own reasons, explained at length above, for knowing that Hankey was out of sympathy with the League of Nations Disarmament policy which Henderson intended to pursue. I had had experience enough of what Cecil called "the power to obstruct and delay" which bureaucrats and militarists could wield. From the first moment I had not the slightest doubt that Vansittart had been jumped up to his new and very powerful office, over senior and better men, in order that he might put spokes in Uncle Arthur's wheels.

Selby's reasons for disliking the appointment were not very different from mine. Ever since the days of Lloyd George's "garden suburb", when Philip Kerr (the Marquis of Lothian) ran a foreign policy of his own from No. 10 Downing Street, Selby had resented strongly the attempts of Prime Ministers or their amateur or professional advisers to upset or override the Foreign Secretary's policies or decisions. It was a subject on which he had unrivalled knowledge and extremely firm convictions. He foresaw trouble from the day that "Van" arrived.

Vansittart was an able man; industrious; devoted, according to his lights, to the national interest; personally likeable and kind.

But, as Permanent Under-Secretary of State to Arthur Henderson, he had two grave defects.

He was a product of the "old diplomacy", and, even more than Crowe, believed in it and shared its prejudices; he never went to Geneva, knew nothing of the League, and cared even less.

Second, he had a passionate obsession about the Germans. For him there were no "good Germans", and never had been. In a wartime book, entitled *Lessons of any Life;* he quoted Tacitus to prove that even the ancient Romans had found the Teutons the least trustworthy and the most barbarous of men.

Already in the 1920s, while Hitler was still a negligible force, and while Gustav Stresemann and the Weimar Republic were relatively strong, and while the League had the declared support of all the Parties in the British state, Vansittart was convinced that we should have another war against the Germans, and have it rather soon. I have no evidence for saying that, consciously or sub-consciously, he *hoped* for such a war, but his views of foreign policy almost suggested that he did.

In any case, he made it very clear that this was the one thing that he saw plainly in the future, and that he thought less than nothing of the hope that the League could prevent it and maintain a lasting peace. His foreign policy objectives were to strengthen British armaments in every way he could; to secure Mussolini, as an ally to fight with us against the Germans; and to educate opinion in Britain and in the Commonwealth, and Empire in a deep distrust, not to say a healthy hatred, of all Germans. As the Second World War drew nearer, his doctrine gained a certain currency, not least in some sections of the Labour Party, and in the war it even influenced Government policy, in most unhappy ways.

Perhaps some readers have begun to say: "Well, dammit, the man was right. We *did* have the war; we had it very soon; we needed much greater armaments; we needed far stronger Allies, especially during the first two years. How right and wise was this Vansittart, and the advice he gave to MacDonald, Henderson, and their Labour colleagues."

I answer at once by quoting Winston Churchill—for the second time; [and his words could come again!] On Cecil's eightieth birthday, in 1944, when the war was nearly won, Churchill wrote Cecil a letter of congratulation, in which he said:

"This war could easily have been prevented, if the League of

Nations had been used with courage and loyalty by the associated nations."[3]

(meaning Britain and France).

"Easily" was his word. What did it mean? That, in Churchill's view, the war need never have happened at all "if the League had been supported with courage and resolution". Sir Robert Vansittart played his own important part in destroying the League. Selby and I had strong ground for apprehension when his appointment was announced.

The London Naval Treaty, 1930

But before this happened, I had been involved in my first important piece of work after my election to Parliament. It was not for Henderson, but for MacDonald.

In 1924 MacDonald kept the Foreign Office for himself, because there was one big over-riding problem in international affairs which needed urgently to be dealt with, and he thought that he could do it—the three fold problem of German reparations, of the French occupation of the Ruhr, and of the embittered relationship of Britain and France. He had convoked a conference in London, had his first contact and co-operation with Edouard Herriot, and had made an outstanding success.

In 1929 he saw that there was another urgent task that needed to be done in international affairs. It was one which he could very properly do as Prime Minister—of course he knew that he could count, not only on the acquiescence, but on the warm support of his Foreign Secretary. The task was to take up the frustrated work of the Coolidge Conference; to make a Treaty of Naval Disarmament which should reduce and limit the strength in cruisers, destroyers and submarines of the Major Fleets; and, not least, to restore cordial relations between Britain and the United States.

The first thing MacDonald had to do was to overcome the opposition of the Admiralty hawks who had inspired Churchill and the Tory Cabinet to wreck the Coolidge Conference in 1927. He called on me to draft the memorandum by which this might be done.

I was in bed one morning not long after MacDonald had returned to

3   Cecil, *All The Way*, p. 234.

No. 10, when my telephone rang, and I heard the Prime Minister himself at the other end. "I want to see you urgently", he said.

"Can you be here at 8.30?"

"Yes, of course", I said with ready optimism—it was 8.10, I had to shave and have a bath, and I was a mile away. But my car was at the door, and the traffic was negligibly light, and as Big Ben Struck eight-thirty I was knocking on the door of No. 10.

The conversation was a pleasure.

The Prime Minister could be charming; he had a quick and fertile mind; he had thought a lot about Disarmament and the cruiser problem. In less than an hour we had agreed on the general lines of what the memorandum ought to say. When I took my draft back the following morning at the same time, MacDonald agreed, after a full discussion, to most of what I had written; but he had some valuable suggestions. So I took my paper back again to my secretary at home (she rejoiced in the family nickname of "Micky Mouse"), and on a third morning visit, MacDonald professed himself as satisfied that the re-drafted memorandum would do what he desired.

I never knew what happened next. The Labour First Lord of the Admiralty was Albert Alexander, a leader of the Cooperative Movement; later, he became an intimate friend; in 1929 we had barely met. But, like MacDonald himself, he was a strong man, and a very successful First Lord in Churchill's Government in the Second World War. In 1929, he backed up MacDonald, the Admiralty opposition was overcome; MacDonald went to Washington to visit Coolidge's Republican successor, President Hoover; Hoover was very keenly for Disarmament; in Washington and New York MacDonald made inspired, and inspiring, speeches—"the speeches of a life-time", someone called them; with Hoover he agreed on all that Coolidge had desired to do.

In January, 1930, Hoover sent an eminent American, Dwight Morrow to London to draw up the Treaty that was required. Morrow was the father-in-law of Charles Lindbergh; he had himself done splendid work as Ambassador to Mexico. The Liberal civilian Government of Japan gave MacDonald and Morrow a very co-operative delegate to help them in their work, the French and the Italians, whom MacDonald had invited, preferred not to come.

Thus it was a three-power conference which drew up the London Treaty of Naval Disarmament.

It was a curious and disjointed conference. MacDonald was (rightly) resolved to do the work himself. But as leader of a minority Government in the House of Commons, it was very difficult for him to attend regular meetings at fixed and normal times. But Mr. Morrow and his Japanese colleague, were very patient; they had to meet at odd hours, and sit around a good deal in their hotels.

In due course, however, the London Treaty was completed, signed and ratified. It made all the reductions and limitations of naval strength that Coolidge had proposed in 1927. Not least important, relations of intimate confidence and friendship were re-established with the United States.

"The Old Adam", and the Sequel

One morning, some time after Vansittart had moved from No. 10, Walford Selby walked across the Private Secretaries' Room from his table in the lefthand corner, to my table in the corner opposite. He had a Foreign Office file in his hand.

"Here, Philip", he said, "You'd better look at this before it goes into Master. I don't think he's going to like it very much."

The file contained a paper by Vansittart, intended for circulation to the Cabinet. It was about the basic principles of British Foreign Policy. I think Vansittart had given it a title: "The Old Adam", but of this I am not sure. That was, in any case, how the paper was always known, and how it can be found, in an amended form, in the Public Record Office today.

As Vansittart first wrote it, it was not a full-blooded hawk's attack on the League of Nations. But it was what he would have called a "realistic" appraisal of the League's weaknesses, and of the frailty of the hope that it could establish lasting peace. It described British interest, and British political and military commitments in every corner of the globe. They could be menaced from many quarters; our power and strength were watched by jealous eyes. We could hope, and work, for peace; but we must be ready also to defend ourselves, our Commonwealth and our Empire, in another war. The League was based on a new idealism, and perhaps that idealism would prevail. But in human nature of foreign statesmen there was still the danger that the Old Adam would emerge—national greed, national arrogance, the inherent aggressive-ness of man, might force us against our will into another conflict even more serious than the last.

In such a crisis, the League might, all too easily, and all too probably fail us in our hour of need. The United States and the Soviet Union were still outside the League, Germany was only partly in. How strong was France, who was always asking for our military guarantee? How strong was the commitment and the cohesion of the other members of the League?

With these sobering thoughts in mind, therefore, we must look to our armaments, and to the men in our armed forces; and we must seek allies on whom we could rely.

There was another policy which might be thought to follow from his argument. Let Britain go all out to strengthen the fabric of the League, to build up the "majesty" of its law, to clarify and organize its sanctions against aggressors who might violate the Covenant and resort to war. By 1930, when Vansittart wrote his paper, the League had stopped four wars and had done so within a week of the day they began and had driven a militarist dictator, Mussolini, from Corfu.

The other Members, in the TMA (Cecil's "Treaty of Mutual Assis-tance") which Hankey had destroyed, in the Geneva Protocol, and since, had shown every disposition to build up the strength of the League, if Britain would only lead them on that way. And the United States was now co-operating in all League conferences; she paid the second largest subscription to its budget after Britain; she was coming closer every day.

This was the policy of Henderson, Vansittart's Secretary of State. But such thoughts did not cross Vansittart's mind. He, like Hankey, looked backwards to the past.

When I had read and had digested the Old Adam, I took some sheets of paper, wrote out my first reaction, and clipped it to the file. Later I often wrote my minutes on the Foreign Office files; at that early stage, and on a memorandum by the Permanent Under-Secretary of State, I thought it wiser to make my observations in a form which Henderson could destroy.

Selby read my minute, then clipped it back onto the file and took it in to Henderson. A long time later, the bell rang for me.

I went in: Henderson held out the file. "Here", he said, "Take this thing down to Van, and get him to make it fit for the Cabinet to read."

I was on amicable terms with Vansittart; I had even played tennis with him, and that always makes a bond.

But I wanted more precise instructions from the Secretary of State before I carried out the delicate but enticing mission which he proposed. So I went over the most important points with Henderson, and ensured that he agreed with what I had written on my bits of paper. So fortified, I went to Vansittart's corner room on the ground floor, and engaged him in what proved to be a long, and not always very satisfactory debate. In the end, he agreed to make some extensive changes in his memorandum, some much against his will. The finished product, as we agreed it, was re-typed, went back to Henderson, and in due course, reached the Cabinet. I did not like it very much, but I thought, and Henderson thought, it could not do much harm.

This was by no means the last occasion on which Vansittart sent up papers designed for the Cabinet or for Cabinet committees, which Henderson did not like. We always went through the same procedure: I wrote my private minute and clipped it to the file; Henderson read it all and rang his bell; I verified that I had understood his thinking and would be sure of his support; and then he said; "Go down to Van. . . . ."

I think Vansittart much disliked the task of re-drafting what he had written in the light of arguments with me. He sought to ridicule it in the Office by dubbing me facetiously "the memorandum king". But on the whole he took it rather well, and we remained on friendly terms.

"On friendly terms". But our views on foreign policy were so very far apart, and we both held them with such ferocity, that we could never appropriately be described as friends; and he could never claim that he had altered my opinions in the least degree.

He was more fortunate with the Parliamentary Under-Secretary of State.

Vansittart, Dalton and the Abyssinian War

Hugh Dalton was a man of violent passions, uncertain temper, great ambition, and real ability. We had been for 3 years at King's together. We had both been members of the secret; but now well-known, if not notorious, society, the Carbonari. Now "well-known", because Dalton, among others, wrote about it; because Rupert Brooke was a founder-member; and because, during Dalton's last year at college, the Society, at its annual dinner, drank the toast: "The King, God damn him".

Of course, the members—there were only a dozen of them—had believed when they drank this disloyal toast—that they were alone in the Fellows' room where the dinner was held. But they were not alone. A spy (a gyp) was hidden behind a curtain, piling up the plates. So next day, the whole college knew just what had happened. The Chetwynd Society (old Etonians and Old Alleynians—why did Eton mix with Dulwich?), champions of the Establishment, sought out Dalton in his rooms, carried him, protesting, to the front court, and threw him, clothes and all, into the fountain.

Why *Dalton*? Because, of all the members of the Carbonari, he was the most ostentatiously a *Socialist*. He did everything to court the unpopularity—some would have said the notoriety—of what was still a proletarian cause.

When he reached the Foreign Office as Parliamentary Under-Secretary of State, he was still flamboyantly a Socialist and a social rebel. He used to tell his fellow members of the House of Commons about an episode of which he was inordinately proud: his father had been Dean of Windsor, and when he, himself, was 4 years old, he had said to Queen Victoria when she came to tea: "Go away, Queen, I don't like you."

Dalton remained flamboyantly a Socialist in the Foreign Office. But he had another foible. He took pride in talking about power-politics, and about how foreign policy could depend on armed strength.

This suited Vansittart very well, and he took great trouble to make friends with Dalton.

But they had another link. They both hated Germans—Dalton ever since German storm-troops had pursued him from the Isonzo and the Piave in 1917.

The link went further. During the First World War, Dalton had been stationed with his battery of field-guns—he was a Lieutenant on the River Isonzo. His battery were attached to the Duke of Aosta's Third

Army, on a sector opposite the Carso, east of Venice. In consequence, he could talk some Italian, and knew something of the Italian Army. Vansittart had a secret plan, which he confided very confidentially to Dalton—he never mentioned it to Henderson or to me. His secret plan was to get Mussolini as an ally in the coming war with Germany. Dalton, who in reality, only half understood the League, was wholly captured by this wonderful idea. But in 1930–5 he sensed the delicacy of the matter, and never talked about it to me or to other Labour Party friends.

After the Labour Government fell from power in August 1931, Vansittart kept up close contact with Dalton. In 1932 he arranged that Dalton should go to Rome to visit Mussolini. The visit was duly carried out, and accomplished everything that Vansittart hoped it would.

Dalton was charmed, and deeply impressed, by Mussolini. He recorded in his diary:

> "6.15.   See the Duce . . . . We spend half-an-hour together . . . . I succeeded in keeping my end up; my Italian is better than usual. He (M.) has charm and intelligence, very small brown eyes . . . . less tall than I expected. But strongly built. He adjusts himself to what he conceives to be my prejudices. He recalls that I have written a book about him. How long was I on their Front? A year and a half, from May 1917, under the Duca d'Hoste.
>
> "I refer to Uncle's (Arthur Henderson's) visit, and say how he returned much impressed with Rome, and with his contact with Mussolini. He doesn't rise at all at this . . . .
>
> "He smiles sweetly. "Yes, why don't you?" almost caressingly, he asks . . . . "Perhaps we have too many old people in high places . . . . Pitt was P.M. at 22." Then I ask him . . . (M. replies: "All Fascists are equal. Work for the state is a duty . . . . When I am next in Rome, I must be sure to come to see him again, he walked me back arm in arm . . . . Yes, charm, intelligence, energy . . . . and play-acting. There is no other living man whom it would have thrilled me more to meet."[4]

---

4   Hugh Dalton's Diary. The above extracts are from entries dated Dec 2, 1932 and Feb 1, 1944. The Diary in Dalton's handwriting is in the Library of the London School of Economics.

There are other sentences in the diary, perhaps more compromising, in view of subsequent events, which Dalton carefully blacked out. But these sentences which I have quoted are enough to show that Dalton was a ready convert to Vansittart's plan. He still called himself a Socialist; but he was so far a power-politics "realist" that he conveniently forgot that Mussolini had destroyed democracy, and that, only a few years before, he had murdered Matteotti, the greatest Socialist, and one of the greatest Europeans of his time—Mussolini had bought a gang of thugs to club Matteotti to death, and to bury his corpse in a wood not far from Rome.

Vansittart was not content with converting Dalton. He wanted to make it impossible for the Labour Party to stand out against his plan. In 1933 he arranged—no doubt the Duce and his Fascists were very glad to help—that Dalton should take Arthur Henderson to Rome to visit Mussolini. Henderson was then, against his will, leader of the Labour Party.[5] If Henderson had understood that all this was to undermine Labour Party opposition to Mussolini's Abyssinian War, he would have died rather than set foot in Rome. But he believed that he was going, as he went to Hitler, to seek Mussolini's help in bringing back life to the Disarmament Conference, which in truth, was already irrevocably dead. Dalton recorded the conversation between the great Disarmer and the criminal dictator who had murdered Greek refuges at Corfu and Matteotti in the streets of Rome: "Uncle played up very well, and he was much impressed."[6]

Vansittart was not concerned with the Labour Party alone. He was no less concerned to square his new Secretary of State, Sir John Simon, the ex-Liberal who was given the Foreign Office in MacDonald's "National" Coalition in October, 1931.

As will be recorded in a later chapter, MacDonald and Simon went to Geneva in March, 1933, to lay a British Draft Disarmament Treaty before the Conference. One of the authors of this Draft Treaty, Major General Temperley, believed that, if they had stayed in Geneva, to push this Treaty through, it might have been accepted, and history changed.[7]

---

5 He was elected leader after the "National" Coalition was formed by MacDonald in 1931. He said to me: "It's a mistake. If they had elected Albert Alexander there would have been two of us."

6 Hugh Dalton's Diary, 1933.

7 Major General Temperley wrote this 3 years later, in 1938. See p. 127 below.

Major General Temperley was a very good judge, none better, of what was possible in the Disarmament Conference.

But MacDonald and Simon resisted the General's entreaties that they should stay on in Geneva. They had received a sudden invitation from Mussolini, of course arranged by Vansittart for the day after McDonald laid his Draft Treaty before the Conference in Geneva, to go on to Rome, to discuss a four-power pact for Europe—a pact between Britain, France, Germany (then meaning Hitler) and Italy (meaning Mussolini), which in practice was intended to replace the League.

This invitation was so timed that the projected Conference in Rome was fixed for 2 days after MacDonald's speech to the Disarmament Conference. It proved irresistible to MacDonald and Simon, as Vansittart, who had arranged it, knew it would.

No sooner had MacDonald made his speech than they packed their bags and took the train to Rome. They left their Draft Disarmament Treaty to its fate, and of course, it perished, as all good hawks had hoped it would.

Their visit to Rome was a huge success, from Vansittart's point of view. They went far towards encouraging Mussolini's Four-Power Pact, which, said its author, would impose peace on Europe "for ten years". They did so, although if they had read the small print, they would have seen that Mussolini was envisaging both the revision of the Treaty of Versailles, and the gradual rearmament of Germany.

But from Vansittart's point of view there was something in the visit to Rome of much greater importance than the projected Four-Power Pact. This was the impression made upon his British guests by the Duce and his Fascist regime.

The Four-Power Pact turned out to be a mirage; before too long, it simply disappeared from view. But MacDonald's and Simon's admiration for Mussolini and for his Government was deep and lasting. When they got back to London, MacDonald gave his Cabinet colleagues "a number of illustrations of the extra-ordinary regeneration of Italy under the Fascist regime"—a regeneration which affected the efficiency of the whole administration and system of government, but had resulted in a widespread spiritual revival among the Italian people.[8]

8   Cabinet Minutes, March 22nd, 1933. Quoted by George Scott, *The Rise and Fall of the League of Nations*, p. 277.

In the light of all that happened to the Italian people in the next 10 years, this judgement shows that in March, 1933, MacDonald was already quite unfit for public office. But to Vansittart it must have been gratifying in no ordinary degree.

But Dalton was the man whom Vansittart most successfully softened up. Arthur Henderson would have been revolted, if he had the smallest inkling of Mussolini's projected Abyssinia War. Not so Hugh Dalton, Vansittart made him quite ready to accept it as the necessary price for an alliance with Fascist Italy.

In January, 1935, when all the diplomatic world had known for 6 months that Mussolini's preparations for the war had been begun, and after Fascist troops, in an unprovoked attack at Wal Wal in southern Abyssinia, had murdered eighteen innocent Abyssinian victims, Konni Zilliacus, then in the Secretariat of the League, wrote to Dalton to alert him to the fact that the aggressor of Corfu was now preparing the invasion, conquest and annexation of the territory of a fellow-Member of the League, Abyssinia, and to urge that the Parliamentary Labour Party should raise the matter in the House of Commons, and should demand a full enquiry on the spot at Wal Wal, and other appropriate action, by the Council of the League.

If Dalton had acted on this timely and far-sighted advice, Mussolini might still have been restrained and the course of history altered. The Peace Ballot campaign had just begun to gain momentum; interest in the League was at a peak; suspicion of the Fascist dictator was universal. The "National" Government, in spite of Hankey and Vansittart, might well have decided to allow the League to pursue its normal course of action by way of a League investigation on the spot at Wal Wal, and the other preventative measures which it could take.

But Dalton would listen to no suggestion that Mussolini should be embarrassed in the execution of his Covenant-breaking plan. He said nothing to his Labour Party colleagues, either in the House of Commons or outside. He said nothing to me, although we sometimes met and discussed international affairs. He wrote to Zilliacus an angry and impatient answer. "Don't think that anybody here will listen to your silly talk about an Abyssinian War. Leave Mussolini alone, and let the League keep quiet," was the snubbing burden of what he wrote.

Zilliacus often spoke to me about this letter in later years, and promised that one day he would show it to me. Unfortunately, he never did so, and unfortunately he destroyed it, with almost all his other papers, before he died. But his widow, Mrs. Janet Zilliacus, conforms that she had seen it, that it had shattered Zilliacus' belief in Dalton, and that its existence and its lamentable content should be published now.

This is by no means the end of the story of what Vansittart did in his long-drawn nefarious campaign to win Mussolini as an ally for Britain in a war against the Germans. I have taken it out of its proper chronological context to show that I was well-advised to feel suspicion of Vansittart's motives in my extensive dealings with him in the years 1929–31. I could sense in almost every conversation his innate, half sub-conscious hostility to the League, and his hankering for the methods of "the old diplomacy" and the "balance of power".

And yet, for all Vansittart's and Dalton's undoubted brainpower, and all Vansittart's well-turned phrases in his memoranda (he was proud of his literary style) the whole concept of an alliance between Britain and Mussolini was childish in its navété.

From his first aggression in Corfu, Mussolini had made it plain that his chief ambition, the consuming ambition of all his years in power, was to build a new Roman Empire by force of arms. When he called the Mediterranean *"mare nostrum"*, he was not only challenging the presence of the British Navy in that historic and romantic sea, and the British Bases at Gibraltar, Malta, Cyprus, Palestine and Alexandria, the Suez Canal; he was sub-consciously revealing the vision of what he hoped that his Fascist Armies would achieve. But it could *only* be achieved at the expense of France and Britain. It was they who held the southern shores of *"mare nostrum"*, and the key bases that could dominate the northern shore as well. It was *their* colonies which could constitute the empire for which he longed. Without these colonies, there was no Empire to be had. Abyssinia, of course—but that was a very minor step to *"mare nostrum"*, and even if he won and held it, his communications with it, his military hold upon it, would be at the mercy of the British, who were in Malta, in Egypt, the Sudan, Somalia, and, worst of all, on the Canal.

So it was always certain that, if Mussolini fought in a Second World War, it would *not* be with France and Britain against the Germans, it would be with the Germans against France and Britain.

This conviction became ever sharper in my mind as I endured the embarrassing but not wholly unenjoyable, conversations with the Permanent Under-Secretary of State when Uncle Arthur rang his bell and said: "Go down to Van."

Long years later, in 1940, terrible events would prove that I was right, and that the "realists", the prophets of power-politics had been dangerously wrong. As I foresaw, with growing certainty and fear, they were ready to sacrifice the League for nothing, for literally nothing, for a mirage that had no reality at all.

De Mortuis, nihil nisi bonum. Do I do right to assault the memory of men who were honest, who believed that they were patriots, and with whom in pre-war years, I remained on reasonably friendly terms?

Yes, I do right. It is a duty to the future to tell the truth about the errors, the follies, and the perverted moral values of the hawks.

CHAPTER 5

The World Disarmament Conference, 1932–1933

The Labour Government's Preparation for the Conference

From the day when he entered the Foreign Office as Secretary of State in the Second Labour Government in May, 1929, Arthur Henderson made it plain that the over-riding purpose of his policy was to secure the execution of the pledges of Article 8 of the League of Nations Covenant and of Part V of the Treaty of Versailles. His purpose was nothing less than the making of a World Treaty of General Disarmament.

Henderson was convinced, as were Robert Cecil, Lloyd George, Smutts, Woodrow Wilson, Charles Hughes, Aristide Briand, Gustav Stresemann, Maxim Litvinoff, and many others among the leading statesmen of the world, that the League could not function as it should, and that probably it would not survive unless the arms race could be ended and the level of world armaments drastically reduced.

Of course, Henderson understood, none better, that it would mean a bitter struggle with the hawks, and that he must mobilize every available ounce of influence on his side.

There were some grounds for optimism.

Since the defeat of the Geneva Protocol, the League of Nations Union had been growing in strength, and it had been conducting a vigorous campaign in favour of Compulsory Arbitration (i.e. British acceptance of the Optional Clause), and general disarmament.

Robert Cecil's resignation over the Coolidge Conference had produced a big effect on general British opinion, and his prestige stood very high.

In the General Election of 1929, which brought the Labour Government to office (although still with a minority in the House of Commons) Cecil had made an appeal to electors of all Parties to forget their usual political affiliations, and to vote for those candidates who pledged themselves most unreservedly to support of the League and general disarmament. In answer to a League of Nations questionnaire, Labour and Liberal candidates gave much stronger pledges of such support than those given by Conservatives. Many electors read these answers and acted on Cecil's advice. Many Members of the new House of Commons were conscious of how much they owed to him.

Some months before the Election, something of great importance had happened. MacDonald had invited Cecil to lunch at the Athenaeum Club, and had asked him whether, if a Labour Government should take office as the result of the Election, he would agree to act as a delegate to Geneva. Cecil had accepted on the spot.

Accordingly, when the Labour Government was formed, MacDonald invited Cecil to No. 10 Downing Street, and renewed his invitation. Cecil again accepted, only making the condition that he must have a room in the Foreign Office. He explained in his book, *A Great Experiment*, that, "unless you are part of the Foreign Office, that distinguished organisation regards you as one of the lesser breeds without the law." MacDonald replied that that must be settled with the Secretary of State.

Henderson was, of course, enraptured to have Cecil's help and support, and I remember vividly how he swept aside some bureaucrats' objections about a room for Cecil in the Office. He was given a very large room, sometimes used for state banquets and receptions, but known in the Office as "The Cabinet Room", because, 30 years before, Cecil's father, Lord Salisbury, when he was Prime Minister and Foreign Secretary, had made it his practice to hold his Cabinet meetings there.

Cecil did not join the Labour Party, and he did not become a Minister of the Crown—his was an honorary appointment, and he received no Government salary. But he performed the same functions that he had performed as Number Two to Austen Chamberlain for the Tory Government, and his influence, in the Foreign Office, with the public, and not least in Geneva, was greater than ever before.

This was due, not only to his great record of achievement and to his leadership of pro-League forces throughout the world, but also to the full confidence which Arthur Henderson gave him from the start. Henderson's admiration for, and trust in, him was fully reciprocated by Cecil, who recorded in *A Great Experiment*, written 12 years later in 1941:

"With him (Henderson) my relations were always perfect . . . . . He was the most successful Foreign Minister we have had since 1918, with no brilliant or showy qualities, but with that faculty for being right which Englishmen, like the Duke of Devonshire of my youth, possess. His political courage was great—almost the rarest and most valuable quality for a statesman."

Cecil's daily collaboration in the Foreign Office and in Geneva was, of course, a great source of strength to Henderson, and a factor of prime importance in the struggle for disarmament, of which Cecil had been for a decade the foremost advocate in the world.

Henderson's team was further strengthened by the fact that William Arnold Forster became Cecil's Secretary and Personal Assistant. Arnold Forster was a famous landscape painter and gardener, with a well-known and beautiful garden in Cornwall. But he was also a well-known authority on League affairs, on arbitration and on disarmament.

He was the son of an outstanding Secretary of State for War in Gladstone's Cabinets. He used to tell how, when he was a boy, his father would show him every year a cheque for many millions of pounds Sterling. (I never fully understood about these cheques, but I know they represented the annual cost to the taxpayer of the British Army, and Arnold Forster spoke of them to illustrate the appalling waste of national resources which armaments involved.)

He was not physically equal to active service in the Armed Forces, but he had been the very successful head of the Blockade Division of the British Admiralty in the First World War. He invented the system of "Navicerts", which greatly increased the effectiveness of the blockade, and greatly reduced the strain on the ships and crews of the Royal Navy.

But the effectiveness of the blockade had weighed very heavily on Arnold Forster's mind; he felt a sense of personal guilt about the German babies and their mothers whom his work had starved to death. To exorcize this feeling, he dedicated himself to the task of ensuring that there should never be another war; he made himself an expert authority on the League, on the arbitration of international disputes, and on Disarmament. His work in the League of Nations Union became of growing importance; his presence in the Foreign Office with Cecil was a strength to the team which Henderson built up.

Pre-Conference Arrangements

Cecil, of course, became the British delegate to the League Preparatory Disarmament Commission, in which not only the leading Members of the League—Britain, France, Germany and Japan—but also the leading non-Members, the United States and the Soviet Union, were strongly represented—the Soviet Union by their very able and distinguished Foreign Minister, Maxim Litvinoff.

The Commission set itself the task of preparing a Draft Treaty of World Disarmament on which the Conference would begin its work.

It sought to make, not a complete Draft, with all the figures of permitted military strength written in—the numbers of men allowed in each signatory nation's armed forces; the numbers of weapons with which each nation's forces could be equipped; the sums of money which each nation might spend in its military budget—but a "skeleton" Treaty, with no such figures of strength written in, but with the model clauses which a Disarmament Treaty should include, and solutions for the technical problems which the reduction and limitation of armaments would necessarily involve.

Some hostile critics, of course, said that, in leaving the Disarmament Conference itself to decide all questions of permitted military strengths, the Commission was shrinking its main task; they said the "skeleton" Treaty would be worthless.

In fact, it was a near miracle that the Commission agreed on any document at all. As in Paris in 1919, it was thanks to Cecil's patience, ingenuity and authority that there was a practical result; without him, there would have been no "skeleton" Treaty, as there would have been no Covenant.

And when, in 1932, the Conference settled down to work, the "skeleton" Treaty proved its great value. All its model clauses were required, and it solved two technical problems of vital importance and great complexity.

It was plain that a Treaty of General World Disarmament would be worth nothing unless it contained a workable and reliable system for reducing and limiting both the manpower and the Budgetary Expenditure of each signatory nation. If a Government could cheat without detection by increasing the number of "effectives" in the forces it maintained, or by spending larger sums of money than the Treaty allowed, the Treaty would inspire no confidence, and, in all probability, it would soon break down.

Neither problem was simple. Some powerful nations—e.g. Britain, the self-governing members of the Commonwealth, the United States—maintained forces which, in all ranks were long-term volunteers, while the majority of nations maintained cadres—General Staffs, Officers and NCO's, who were long-term volunteers, while other ranks were short-term conscripts. The system of manpower reduction and limitation, like the system of budgetary reduction and limitation, had to apply to both types of forces, and had also to limit the number of "trained reserves" who could be mobilized at the outbreak of war.

After long months of work the Commission solved the manpower problem by a device which limited the number of "effectives' man-days with the colours", and the Conference discovered when it met that the system which the Commission had worked out would meet all the requirements of a Treaty of World Disarmament.

The problem of budgetary reduction and limitation was even more difficult. But the Commission, with the expert help of Mr. Per Jacobsson of the League Secretariat, worked out a scheme which the Conference decided would enable League financial inspectors to discover any cheating at a very early stage.

Both plans, for Manpower and Military Budgets,[1] could be adopted for a World Disarmament Treaty in 1978, if one should be made. If Disarmament ever comes about, Cecil's League Preparatory Commission will have played its vital part.

Henderson, meanwhile, had other preoccupations. As Cecil noted in one of his books,[2] Henderson had already, in the Assembly of 1929, become a leader in Geneva, as he had been in 1924.

1   In 1978 inflation and rapidly changing rates of international exchange have introduced complications into the Budgetary Limitation Scheme, these have been dealt with by a group of Experts appointed by Dr. Kurt Waldheim, the Secretary General of the United Nations.

2   Cecil, *A Great Experiment*, p. 200.

In due course, he persuaded the Council to fix the date of the Disarmament Conference—already long overdue, as the authors of Article 8 of the Covenant would have thought. The date chosen was February 6th, 1932—i.e. a further long delay to allow the League Secretariat and the Governments to make their final preparations. Looking back, I have little doubt that hawks of different nations, including, perhaps, *German* hawks, had a hand in imposing this further long delay. But I remember no specific evidence on this point; I only remember a sense of relief and excitement that, after 12 years of waiting and hoping, a date had at last been fixed for the Conference to meet. But, again, looking back, it seems clear that the chances of success would have been much greater if the date fixed had been February, 1931, or even October, 1930, rather than 1932.

Another question which Henderson had to solve was that of the Presidency.

Cecil was in favour of choosing Edouard Benes, then Foreign Minister of Czechoslovakia, to be the President. Perhaps, if Gustav Stresemann had been alive to speak for Germany, this might have been agreed.

But Stresemann was no longer there. In August, 1929, in the Conference at The Hague (Scheveningen) he had, with the help of Henderson and Briand, secured the withdrawal of Allied Forces from the Occupation of the Rhineland, 5 years before the date which the Treaty of Versailles laid down. Having secured this triumph for his policy of "fulfillment" of the Peace Treaty, he went on, as Henderson and Briand did, to the Tenth Assembly of the League.

He had been very ill while he was negotiating at The Hague. In Geneva it was clear that he was sinking fast. Nevertheless, with characteristic moral and physical courage, he inscribed himself to speak on an early day in the opening General Debate of the Assembly. When he mounted the speaker's rostrum, he was already struggling; every 10 minutes he had to stop to drink a cordial which his doctors had prescribed; after every sentence, he was gasping for breath. I was sitting very close in front of him, and I could see what every painful effort was costing him. The packed Assembly audience, delegates, press and public, listened with rapt attention to every syllable; they understood that it was the last speech which he would ever make.

In spite of every difficulty, he made his whole declaration from first to last—a declaration of burning faith in peace and international co-operation. He was utterly exhausted, and his hearers were profoundly moved, when he sat down. Three weeks later—before the Assembly ended—he was dead.

The loss of Gustav Stresemann was a grievous blow to Weimar Germany, to the Council and Assembly of the League; above all, to the cause of World Disarmament. His wisdom and authority would have been a great asset to the Conference in 1932.

His successor as German Foreign Minister, Dr. Curtius, was a liberal and upright man. But he had neither the genius nor the national and international standing of Gustav Stresemann. He had not the strength to accept Benes as President of the Conference. Czechoslovakia had a military alliance with France—an alliance which France betrayed in 1938. For German chauvinists, the fact of the alliance ruled Benes out; Henderson himself proved to be the man for whom unanimous approval could be obtained; Henderson was invited by the Council to be the President of the Conference.

Of course the hawks everywhere attacked the nomination. "Henderson cannot be an impartial President", declared a reactionary Prime Minister in the French Chamber; "he is known to be in favour of Disarmament". But the Council of the League thought otherwise, and the world in general approved their choice. The omens all seemed propitious as the Conference drew near.

The Work of the Militarist Saboteurs

We were all acutely conscious in the British Foreign Office that there were hawks in many countries—men who thought the League and Disarmament were utopean nonsense, and who shared Hankey's conviction that "whatever you do, war will come". We had some in the Foreign Office itself; Vansittart showed clearly that his belief in World Disarmament was less ardent than ours.

As explained at many points above, the attitude of Britain was all too likely to be decisive in the Conference, and in due course events proved that that was true. And the prospects for British support for

World Disarmament changed suddenly and sharply for the worse in 1931.

In October of that year—4 months before the Conference was due to meet—Ramsay MacDonald handed to King George V the resignation of his Labour Government, and then accepted from the King a mandate to form a new Government, a so-called "National" Coalition, in which most of the leaders of the three Parties agreed to serve. MacDonald was joined in this Government by three prominent members of his Labour Cabinet.

In the General Election which followed, Labour lost 240 seats in the House of Commons. Among those defeated were Henderson and almost every other Labour Minister who had not joined MacDonald. A large number of the Tory Members elected to the House of Commons cared nothing for the League or for Disarmament; the new Foreign Secretary, Sir John Simon, was to prove himself a redoubtable opponent; the "Service" Ministers—Douglas Hogg (the first Lord Hailsham), Secretary of State for War; Commander Eyres-Monsell, First Lord of the Admiralty; the Marquis of Londonderry, Secretary of State for Air—were all ardent hawks, and they had other supporters in the Cabinet.

The other—non-governmental—categories of hawks were very active in their work against Disarmament. Some private manufacturers of arms were loud in their support of Hitler, and declared that we must let him re-arm Germany, in order that he might destroy the Bolsheviks in Russia. They did not hesitate to advertise their tanks in German journals, although Germany was forbidden to own or purchase tanks by the Treaty of Versailles. When Hitler came to power, they did not hesitate to sell him the latest type of British tank and the latest British aero-engine—in aero-engines Britain then, as now, led the world.[2]

The private manufacturers did not hesitate to subsidize the so-called "Patriotic Societies",[3] and to encourage them to work against Disarmament.

This sinister support for the military-industrial complex had some importance, since it created the illusion of public support for the militarist Ministers in the Government. How little real support they had

2 Philip Noel-Baker, *The Private Manufacture of Armaments*, p. 195.
3 Philip Noel-Baker, ibid., p. 331.

among the general public was shown by the Peace Ballot in 1934–5 (see pp. 138–141). Two examples of the attitude of these Patriotic Societies may be quoted:

A statement given to me by a pilot after he had paid a visit to the most important of the Air Lobby Societies:

"I called at the office of the Air League of the British Empire . . . . . to enquire about the aims and objects of the Air League and its members.

"In the course of conversation, I said to the man who was interviewing me: 'What about the other Societies, like the Royal Aeronautical Society? Are you in competition with each other, or do you all work together?' He answered: 'Well, as a matter of fact, there used to be a good deal of jealousy and rivalry, but now, in face of the common enemy, Disarmament, we are all as thick as thieves'."

Yet another Air Society, "The Hands Off Britain Air Defence League", made a house-to-house distribution of an expensive pamphlet about the perils of air attack in the next war, and the need to build a great "New Winged Army of Long Range British Bombers to smash the Foreign Hornets in their Nests." A would-be patriot wrote to the Director of this second League, expressing the desire to join, and enquiring what subscription should be paid. The Director answered:

"Dear Sir

I thank you for your letter, and I have much pleasure in sending you a leaflet in connection with our campaign. Please do not trouble to subscribe anything at all, but if you can get up a meeting locally, it will indeed be a great help."

No subscriptions needed to finance the great campaign! It was subsequently shown that this Society was receiving large-scale financial gifts from the manufacturers of military aircraft.[4]

The French Private Manufacturers of Arms were even more active than their British colleagues. Since before the First World War, the most important French newspaper, *Le Temps*, had been under the control of the Comité des Forges, that is, of the Private Arms Manufacturers of France.

---

4   I guarantee the authenticity of these two documents, which I printed in 1936 in *The Private Manufacture of Armaments*. See that work, pp. 321–45.

In 1930, the Comité bought control of *Les Debats*, the second most important organ of political opinion in France. It was freely said in Paris that the Comité had also acquired control of most of the other newspapers and journals of Paris.

Through these organs of the Press, the Comité conducted a merciless campaign of invective and slander against Aristide Briand and his policy of support for the League and World Disarmament.

They succeeded in defeating Briand's attempt to bring France and Italy into the London Treaty of Naval Disarmament.

In 1931–2 they defeated Briand's candidature for the Presidency of the French Republic, and elected instead a political nonentity, Senator Lebrun, the candidate of the Comité des Forges.[5]

The Minister of War of France and first French delegate to the Conference when the Disarmament Conference opened in February, 1932, was Monsieur Tardieu, whose contacts with the Comité des Forges were known to be extremely close.

Even more serious was the work of the hawks in Germany.

The Treaty of Versailles forbade the great firm of Krupps, and all the other private arms firms in Germany, to manufacture armaments or ammunition of any kind.

So Krupps began to manufacture sewing machines in their works at Essen.

But their Chairman, Hugenberg, used the vast profits they had made in the First World War to build up a greater empire of the media than any private firm had ever built before. The Hugenberg Konzern bought more than half of all the daily newspapers in Germany. It bought *all* the Press Advertising Agencies—so that the daily papers which it did not buy could be starved of advertisements, if they wrote things that Hugenberg did not approve.

It bought *Die Woche* and the other leading weekly and monthly periodicals.

It bought the great German Film Enterprise, UFA, and the new Radio Broadcasting Service.

It threw all this vast network of opinion-forming agencies into a sustained attack on the Treaty of Versailles, on Disarmament, and on

5   The facts justifying these statements are given at length in *The Private Manufacture of Armaments*, pp. 346 et seq.

the leading prophet of liberal democracy, Stresemann. To this end, it threw the full weight of its support behind the unknown Austrian proletarian, Adolf Hitler. It is safe to say that, without the Hugenberg Konzern, Hitler would have remained a fanatical nonentity.

As it was, the Nazi Movement gathered strength as, year after year, the Hugenberg propaganda assaulted the ears and the minds of the German public. In 1929 the world slump robbed seven million Germans of their work—the young men could find no jobs as they left school or college.[6] The manufacturers of arms—Krupp, Thyssen, Stinnes and many more—gave Hitler vast sums of money to pay the volunteers in his private armies, the SA and SS. Gradually the whole democratic structure of the Weimar Republic was undermined. In January 1933, half-way through the League Disarmament Conference in Geneva, a traitorous Chancellor, the militarist General Schleicher, induced the aged President of the Republic, Field-Marshal Hindenburg, to name Hitler as Chancellor of the Reich. Of course, in all this, Hugenberg, Krupp and Co. had had the help and the support of the German General Staff, and of many reactionary militarist officials in Government Departments. But essentially Hitler was the creature of the vested armament interests, whose purpose was simple but terrible—to smash the League of Nations and re-arm Germany.

There is ample evidence that throughout the whole of their campaign, the German militarists never had the support of the majority of the German people, and if I had the space, I could bring conclusive evidence that Hitler never won it after he came to power.

I could tell much more of the preparations made by hawks in many countries to defeat the Disarmament Conference. What follows will show the sinister importance of the scattered scraps of evidence which I have summarized above.

6   In the summer of 1930, Cecil visited the University of Heidelberg. A Professor told him that of a class of 150 students who had graduated 12 months before, 3 had then found jobs; one as a clerk, one as a shop assistant, and one cleaning the stables of a herd of cows.

CHAPTER 6

The NGOs Disarmament Campaign—1929–1932

Cecil knew that the hawks would be extemely active, and would be very hard to beat. He relied on the power of world opinion, and set himself to organize a great international campaign of education.

He thought that, in this campaign, British opinion must take the lead. As he was not a Minister in the Labour Government he was free to go on acting as Chairman of the British League of Nations Union. At his instigation, the Union threw its full resources into a sustained effort to make the British people understand why it was vital that the pledges of Article 8 of the Covenant should be fulfilled.

Every one of the Union's more than 600 local Branches took its full part in this campaign. They received a constant stream of admirable briefing material—some written with authority by Arnold Forster—from LNU headquarters—pamphlets, leaflets, posters, articles in the Union's journal, *Headway*, which had a circulation of more than 80,000. There were many hundreds of meetings, often with speakers of national repute; the meetings were widely reported in the local and the national Press; the reports were followed up by a stream of letters to the Editors, who were glad to print them. I travelled far and wide to these meetings, and I have a vivid memory of the keenness of the audiences, of the lively question-times, and of the vigorous debates which sometimes ensued.

I remember, too, the pressure which Union branches brought to bear on their local MPs. It was not the least effective part of the campaign.

But Cecil did not only work on the LNU alone. He formed a

national Disarmament Committee, and brought together leaders of Non-Governmental Organizations of many kinds.

Since his Oxford days, he had been a close personal friend of Cosmo Lang, the Archbishop of Canterbury, and Lang used his great influence to give Cecil strong Church support. With Anglicans in the lead, Roman Catholics, Methodists, Presbyterians, Quakers and other Free Churches furnished local leaders for co-ordinating Committees, and a strong body of supporters from their congregations.

Cecil's relations with the trade unions were always good, and in seeking their co-operation, he was helped by Henderson, the most outstanding trade unionist in Parliament. The Trades Union Congress sent national leaders to sit on Cecil's Disarmament Committee. Individual unions gave subscriptions to the funds, and printed a whole series of feature articles in their respective journals. In these ways, the campaign reached many millions of organized workers.

The Co-operative Movement gave similar assistance. Through their local societies, their educational services, their women's guilds, and their many publications, they reached as many individual members as the trade unions.

All the women's organizations took part—the Women's International League for Peace and Freedom ("the WIL"), the Women's Institutes, the Townswomen's Guild, and the rest.

So did the Rotary Clubs, many Chambers of Commerce, the universities and technical colleges, and very many schools.

There were also many broadcast discussions on the BBC.

The campaign came to a climax in a meeting, in July, 1931, in the London Albert Hall—a public meeting attended by 10,000 people, and in many ways unique in the annals of British politics.

The chief speakers at the meeting were three Prime Ministers—Ramsay MacDonald, then in office; David Lloyd George, the Prime Minister whose leadership did so much to win the First World War; and Stanley Baldwin, Prime Minister in 1922–3, 1924–9, and again in 1936. They were then the leaders of the three great Parties in the State.

The Chairman of the meeting was Field Marshal Sir William Robertson, a Scotsman always known as "Wullie"—the only man in the history of the British Army who rose from being a "private" soldier to the top rank of the supreme command. "Wullie" had been Chief of the

Imperial General Staff ("CIGS") for three decisive years of defeat and victor in the First World War (1915–18). "Wullie's" prestige was equal to his experience of war. He caused a sensation in the Albert Hall, and it carried great weight with the British public, when he opened the meeting with the following words:

"Ten million lives were lost to the world in the last War, and they say that £70 million in money was spent in the preliminary bombardment in the Battle of Ypres; before any infantry left their trenches the sum of £22 million was spent, and the weight of ammunition fired in the first few weeks of that Battle amounted to 480 thousand tons. . . . . I do not believe that that represents the best use the world can be expected to make of its brains and its resources. I prefer to believe that the majority of people in the world in these days think that war hurts everybody, benefits nobody—except the profiteers, and settles nothing.

"As one who has passed pretty well half a century in the study and practice of war, I suggest to you that you should give your support to Disarmament, and so do your best to ensure the promotion of peace."[1]

This speech was a smashing blow at the hawks who were seeking to spread alarm, despondency and defeatism about the Disarmament Conference, which was due to meet in 6 months' time.

Its effect was enhanced by the three Prime Ministers, who all argued the case for the early and effective fulfilment of Article 8 of the Covenant.

But when Cecil moved the vote of thanks to the speakers, it was *he* who received the loudest cheer of the day from the audience that had over-filled the Albert Hall.

The meeting was the first in Britain to be recorded on video-tape; the film was shown and re-shown to innumerable audiences in cinemas throughout the land. Britain was alerted to the coming Conference, and to what it ought to do.

But Cecil's campaign was not confined to Britain alone.

In 1930 he was elected to be the President of the International Federation of League of Nations Societies,[2] in that capacity, he

1   Albert Hall, London, July 11th, 1931.
2   Now transformed into the World Federation of United Nations Association (WFU-NA) whose present Secretary-General is Mr. Frank Field of Britain.

organized an International Disarmament Committee, in which the lead-
ing international NGOs combined their efforts: the World Council of
Churches, powerful organizations of the Roman Catholic Church; the
International Federation of Trade Unions (40 million paying members),
led by Léon Jouhaux, with whom Cecil had worked in Geneva; the
International Co-operative Alliance, 85 million *families*, and very strong
in 70 countries from Finland to Ceylon—Tanner of Finland was their
President; the Women's Movements, and many more.

The Women's Organizations, national and international, had
joined together in intensive, co-ordinated educational work. Not the
least of their activities was the mounting of the biggest international
petition there has ever been; nothing approaching it in scale was ever
tried, before or since.

All these movements, together with the international organizations
of teachers, students, rotarians and other sections of society, had carried
out an educational programme for three full years by the time the
Conference met in February, 1932. They had done so through their
innumerable newspapers and periodicals, through their local branches
at the grass-roots level, and through their regional, national and international conferences.

In most countries by 1932, men and women were talking in mines
and factories, in banks and clubs and universities and schools, in shops
on land and ships at sea, about football, dogs and horses and their
children, as they always do—but *also* they were talking about disarmament, why it mattered, what air bombardment was going to mean if
there should be another war. The whole world was conscious of the
problem; aware that the Conference was soon to meet; concerned,
anxious, that it should not fail.

To one movement's informed and vigorous support Henderson
attached particular importance—that of the Labour and Socialist International, of which he had been President.

The International were due to hold a major Congress in Vienna in
July, 1930.

Vienna was then the Mecca of Social Democratic pilgrims from
many lands. Its Social Democratic City Council, with the leadership of
the famous Burgermeister Seitz, had carried through programmes of
housing, school construction, social services and public parks that were

the admiration of the world. In great measure they had defeated the international economic slump that was destroying parliamentary institutions both in European countries and elsewhere. This meant that the Congress was certain to attract a large attendance, and to command the attention of the Press.

Henderson had arranged with the Executive Committee of the International that they should lay a strong and comprehensive Resolution on Disarmament before the Congress. But he felt that, as British Foreign Secretary, he should not himself attend a Party Congress, or move the Resolution, as normally he would have wished to do. But he thought the Resolution ought to have a *British* stamp, so he got the Executive Committee to agree that *I* should move it in his stead.

He knew my thinking on the subject was identical with his; we had been discussing it every day for many months. So much so, that he did not even ask to see my speech before I made it. In fact, I only began to work out what I should say *after* I had left Victoria Station, and I made my notes in my compartment in the sleeping car that took me from Paris to the Austrian capital.

Of course, when the day came for the Disarmament debate in the Congress, I was hideously nervous. The hall where the Congress met seemed to me immensely large; every seat from floor to roof was filled; I had no idea how many of the audience would understand my English; I had a great deal that I *had* to say, but it was *imperative*, above all else, that I should not speak too long. To compound my worries, there was a heatwave; as I sat and waited for the Chairman to call me, I felt that I was melting to pulp.

It was even worse when I had been called—my chief memory of my speech is that I perspired so freely that I must have lost a stone. But, fortunately, I was used to speaking in big halls; I spoke more slowly than I should have done at home; I was very well prepared; and the audience were marvellous—they sat so still that it seemed to me that every single man or woman was understanding every word I said.

Of course, they were highly sophisticated people; they understood that for Germany, and therefore for Austria as well, it would almost certainly mean a Nazi coup if the Disarmament Conference should be allowed to fail. They knew, too, as did the Press, that everything I said had the full approval of the British Secretary of State for Foreign Affairs.

That was why they were enduring the suffocating heat with such fortitude; that was why they welcomed what I said with loud and prolonged applause.

Of course, I had made a strong demand for drastic World Disarmament; and I had made it plain that Henderson, and the Labour Government, and the vast majority of the British people, were resolved to bring that World Disarmament about.

The Congress of the Socialist International liked what I said, and they gave it warm approval. The Press of Europe reported it as though it had been Henderson himself who spoke; it was front page news in every paper.

But for me the speech had been like an Olympic final; I had had to give it everything I had. And when at last the Congress rose for lunch, I felt that I had reached the limit of my endurance. Scouting the thought of food, I made with all speed for a (Social Democratic) swimming bath near by. I laid my clothes out in the blazing sun to dry; spent an hour or more in the water, swimming; by the time the Congress reconvened, I felt almost new again. Then, my duty done, I danced every evening for a week to the lovely music of the Austrian bands—*then* (alas, not *now*) the finest dance bands in the world.

Of course, after the Disarmament debate, the Congress had voted, with no dissentient voice, for the Resolution which Henderson had proposed—the commitment of the Socialist International to his policy was unanimous and complete.

There was one other movement to whose support Henderson attached almost equal importance—that of the Ex-Servicemen, the Veterans, the Anciens Combattants, of the First World War. His three sons had all served at the Front in the British Army; one, the eldest had been killed; the other two, Will and Arthur, Junior, were in 1929 to 1931 Members of the House of Commons.

The Veterans were organized in two International Federations, popularly known as FIDAC and CIAMEC. Between them they claimed to speak for 8 million of their comrades who had fought and had survived, and for 10 million other comrades who had fought and died.

The two Federations had never worked together on any subject since the War had ended in 1918. Only Disarmament brought them together. Thanks to a splendid leader of their movement, Rene Cassin of

France, they *did* send a joint deputation to the League Disarmament Conference to demand that the Governments should not let it fail. But Cassin's plan was on so grandiose a scale that it was March, 1933, before his Deputation could be assembled in Geneva. When it came it was as magnificent and as impressive as Cassin had hoped—something that those who saw it never forgot. But, like the Conference itself, it had been delayed too long. I will describe it, and its success and failure, a little later on.

The Conference Set-Backs

The success of this pre-Conference educational campaign was a great encouragement to Cecil and Henderson. They both said to me that what happened in Geneva would depend on the Strength of public opinion in support of Disarmament, and on how fiercely that support would be maintained if set-backs and disappointments should occur. They were not afraid of public indifference when the Conference first met; they both feared disillusion and defeatism if a good result was long delayed.

There were set-backs, very grievous set-backs, before the Conference met.

When the opening date was fixed for February 6th, 1932, Henderson was Secretary of State for Foreign Affairs, and he had firmly established his authority both at home and abroad.

Cecil had then been the British delegate to the Preparatory Disarmament Commission, and it was plain that Henderson would invite him to lead the British Delegation to the Conference.

Briand was still Foreign Minister of France, and perhaps the most powerful spokesman for Disarmament in the world.

Nansen had promised Cecil that he would be the Delegate of Norway to the Conference; that he would stay the whole time, and that he would use his great influence with delegates, press and public in support of whatever proposal for armament reduction Cecil might put forward. Nansen often told me in the late twenties that, with each passing year, Disarmament was becoming more important. He was convinced that the fate of democracy in Germany, the fate of the League, and the avoidance of another World War, would depend on the faithful fulfilment of Article 8 of the Covenant and of Part V of the Treaty of Versailles. As opportunity after opportunity for Disarmament was missed, he became increasingly anxious, and increasingly resolved to do everything he could to bring it about.

But before the appointed date arrived, February 6th, 1932, a series of disasters had occurred.

The British Labour Government had fallen from power; Henderson was no longer Secretary of State; he had been replaced by Sir John Simon.

In consequence, Cecil would no longer be the leader of the British Delegation to the Conference. He would be a private citizen, helplessly watching Simon and others failing to do what was required.

Briand was no longer the Foreign Minister of France; he lay dying in his country home away from Paris.

And Nansen was dead. His magnificent life had been ended by a heart attack, due to 10 years of over-work in the service of the League of Nations. The voice that would have moved the Conference and roused the world had been forever stilled.

These were all grave disasters.

The gravest was, perhaps, the choice of Simon as Foreign Secretary.

Simon was a life-long Liberal, with Liberal instincts and desires. He had held high office in a British Liberal Government a quarter-of-a-century before. In 1932, beyond all doubt, he *wanted* a Disarmament Treaty, and for some time worked hard and skilfully to get it.

But in joining the MacDonald-Stanley Baldwin "National" Coalition he had been guilty of a great betrayal of his Liberal principles and his Liberal friends. He had always been a staunch Free Trader; but, tempted by the offer of the Foreign Office, he had swallowed the Tory heresy of "Tariff Reform" (i.e. a policy of high Tariff Protection for British industries) and, in effect, this meant that he became a Tory, or at least the prisoner of the 550 reactionary Tories who supported the "National" Coalition in the House of Commons.

Simon's career in Geneva was to show that, if he could swallow Tariff Reform, he could swallow anything, including the recantation of his own best work. And it was disastrous.

But the other disasters were serious, too. Henderson retained the respect, and, indeed, the affectionate regard of the Delegates; but his authority was evidently diminished by his loss of office, and on occasions this was very serious indeed.

The absence of Cecil, Briand, and Nansen left the Conference without strong leaders. They were all men of iron nerve, and iron nerve was needed to take decisions about armaments and national defence. Moments were to come in the Conference when their leadership, their eloquence and their debating skill might well have been decisive in securing the right result.

Vox Populi

These set-backs were in some degree redeemed by what happened at the opening session of the Conference.

Henderson persuaded the Bureau of the Conference that, before the Delegates began their opening General Debate, they should hear spokesmen of the international non-governmental organizations which had played the leading parts in Cecil's international disarmament campaign.

There was no precedent in the history of diplomatic or other international Congresses for such a course. Inevitably there were traditionalists in the Bureau who opposed it, and I thought, at more than one moment in the discussion, that the proposal would be lost. But Henderson's personal influence prevailed, and the resulting demonstration proved to be an event of real importance. Even most of those who had opposed it, later confessed that they had been wrong.

The speakers were impressive personalities, and together their organizations had a total of more than a thousand million regularly subscribing members—a constituency in 1932 of almost half the individuals who then made up the human race, and a good deal more than half the adults.

Pride of place in this opening Conference session was given to the women, whose organizations had brought a monster petition signed by people in many differenct countries.

An American lady, Miss Mary Dingman,[1] Chairman of the Geneva

1   The 15 Womens' Organisations, over whose Joint Consultative Committee Miss Dingham presided, had a joint membership of forty-five million (45,000,000).

Women's Co-ordinating Committee, explained the many different activities they had undertaken in their long-term educational campaign; and then gave the Conference assurances about the value and the integrity of their petition. Everywhere they had taken great trouble to ensure that no one under 18 years of age should sign it; that no one should sign it twice; and that everyone should understand its meaning and its purpose *before* they signed.

Then women representatives of their various movements entered in pairs, carrying between them large baskets containing the sheets of signatures from their respective countries. Many of the women were in national dress, and they made an attractive and a picturesque group as they lined up in front of the President's platform. Altogether their petitions bore the signatures of more than twelve million adult citizens who demanded that the Conference should disarm the world and so establish peace.

Then came the speakers on policy. Cecil, as President of the World Federation of League of Nations Societies, then large and influential bodies in many countries; Emile Vandervelde, former Prime Minister of Belgium, and President of the Labour and Socialist International (affiliated members 39 million); Léon Jouhaux of France, leader of 40 million members of the International Federation of Trade Unions; Tanner of Finland, President of the International Co-operative Alliance, whose members included 85 million *families*; a Roman Catholic lady from Latin America who spoke for 400 million organized women members of the Roman Church; James Green of Yale University, U.S.A., who spoke movingly for the students of the world, the cannon-fodder of the next World War, if there should be one.

Cecil was the first to speak and there were many in his audience who thought it poetic justice that his should be the first voice to expound the hopes and the demands of the thousand million. For without Cecil, as Woodrow Wilson wrote to him in 1919, there would probably have been no Covenant; without him, there would have been no agreement on Article 8, which laid on the League the duty to carry through Disarmament; without his leadership in the Assembly and the Council of the League, those institutions might never have come to real, effective life. From the First League Assembly onwards, he had laboured tirelessly to keep Disarmament at the top of the international agenda, and to prepare the documents from which the Conference was to start. He had inspired the masses for whom he was to plead, and most of his hearers thought that, but for him, the Conference would never have met at all. It was right that the first word should be his.

But there was irony in the thought that, with all this record of constructive planning and achievement to his credit, this first speech in the Conference should also be his last. He was not to sit among the Delegations on the floor. He would mount the platform, make one speech, leave the platform and be gone. The greatest expert and the greatest leader on the subject, he would watch in silent impotence in London what other, lesser, men would make of the great opportunity that had been created, principally by him.

His speech was worthy of the great occasion. He was in his finest form.

The power and clarity of his argument were so convincing that almost every delegate who spoke in the General Debate referred to him, and much more important, his thesis came to dominate the proceedings of the Conference from first to last.

Here a brief summary of what he said will suffice, with an account of the remarkable effect which it produced.

Cecil's thesis was a concise but comprehensive exposition of the Disarmament policy for which he had secured the approval and support of the World Federation of League of Nations Societies.

In formulating this policy, Cecil and the Federation began from the fundamental question that should be the starting point of every consideration of armaments, strategy and war:

What are armaments for?

Answer: The function of armaments is national defence; and, in a League of Nations world, in which the law of the Covenant prevails, national defence is their *only* legitimate purpose. The objective of a World Disarmament Convention should, therefore, be to reduce the armaments of all the Signatory Powers to what they need for national defence, and to abolish forces and weapons which would help *offensive*, i.e. aggressive warlike operations.

The recent experience of the First World War had proved that some forces and some weapons help defence, while others help *offence* i.e. help to overcome defence.

For four years, along a front of 400 miles, across the North of Europe, rifles, machine-guns and small calibre mobile field artillery had made trenches, and barbed wire entanglements and concrete pill-boxes impregnable against the heaviest and the most resolute attack. For 4 years, no Commander on either side had been able to advance more than a few hundred yards, no matter how many thousands of lives he sacrificed. The rifles, machine-guns and light mobile field artillery of both sides proved defensive in a very high degree.

But in the later stages of the War, the General Staffs were persuaded to introduce tanks and heavy mobile artillery, and bombing aircraft. The heavy guns and bombers demolished the barbed wire, the trenches and even the pill-boxes; the tanks defied rifle and machine-gun fire. They proved to be what Liddell Hart called them: "Defence breaking weapons", that is, they helped *offensive* operations to succeed.

Similarly, battleships of over 10,000 tons displacement, aircraft carriers and submarines helped offensive operations at sea.

And experience had shown that all military aircraft could help powerfully to overcome national defence.

Starting from the fundamental principle that the only legitimate function of armaments is national defence, Cecil accordingly proposed that all the signatory parties to a Disarmament Treaty should make large and progressive reductions in the manpower of their armed forces, and should abolish the weapons which were primarily efficient for *offence*; tanks, heavy mobile guns, poison gases; battleships of over 10,000 tons displacement, aircraft carriers and submarines; all military and naval aircraft, and all air forces.

If this were done, he argued, the burden of armaments would be greatly lightened for every nation, great or small; the national defence of every nation would be greatly strengthened; the risk of aggressive Covenant-breaking, surprise attack would be reduced; the League would be given more time to secure the settlement of international disputes. "Confidence" and stability in international affairs would be increased.

Cecil's argument was reinforced by Emile Vandervelde, the first Social Democratic Prime Minister of Belgium; he spoke with passion; his country had been the victim of aggression in 1914.

The last of the other spokesmen of the NGOs was James Green, the student; he stirred the conscience of the Ministers, who knew that the fate of Green's generation would depend on the outcome of the work they did in the Conference. Before Green had finished, everybody in the Conference Hall had understood that the vast majority of the human race would be watching what happened there, and would be demanding that the debates should inaugurate a new and glorious epoch in man's affairs.

One Delegate more than others had been impressed by Cecil's case. This was Simon, the new British Foreign Secretary, who arrived in Geneva with the prestige of the "National" Government's massive victory in the General Election, and with the enormous influence of the British Empire, behind him. Everybody knew from the first day that it might well be in Simon's power to decide whether the Conference should succeed or fail.

Simon was a strange man. He had great intellectual and forensic gifts, not matched, alas, by moral power. As a French friend said to me in those early weeks—I think it was the witty Sacha Grumbach: "Within a week of Henderson's arrival in Geneva, he had won everybody's confidence and trust; within a week of Simon's arrival, no-one believed a word he said." Grumbach—if it was Grumbach—went on to say that Simon "seemed to have no principles except the principle to have no principles." Perhaps that was unfair. For at least he was guided by the principle that, at every cost, John Simon should remain the Foreign Secretary.

But Simon was deeply impressed by Cecil's speech. No doubt as the result of his past association with Liberal friends, he found that he really *wanted* Disarmament to succeed. He knew it would be a thorny task to make some of his Tory colleagues in the "National" Coalition agree to any measure of armament reduction. But he thought that they would find it very hard to resist Cecil's plan for strengthening national defence by abolishing the forces and weapons of offence. He understood the powerful arguments he could use to support that plan; he did not see what valid arguments opponents of disarmament could use against it.

So he went far towards endorsement of the plan in his first speech in the Conference General Debate. He pursued the matter in the General Commission of the Conference. (The General Commission was a Committee of the whole, in which the leaders of the national Delegations sat.)

He talked a lot about the plan in private conversations, and invented a new name for it; he called it "Qualitative Disarmament".

After some weeks he moved a Resolution in the General Commission which committed the Conference in general terms to the principle of "Qualitative Disarmament".

The Resolution was unanimously accepted—a preliminary triumph for both Simon and for Cecil.

A little later he moved a second Resolution which advanced matters an important stage further:

"In seeking to apply the principle of Qualitative Disarmament, the Conference is of the opinion that the range of land, sea, and air armaments should be examined by the competent Special Commissions with a view to selecting those weapons whose character is most specifically offensive, or those most efficacious against national defence or most threatening to civilians."

The "Special Commissions" were the Naval, Land and Air Commissions which the Conference had decided to set up. Whereas for the most part the Delegates in the General Commission were Ministers or other politicians, in the Special Commissions, most of the representatives were high-ranking Staff Officers, Admirals, Generals, or Air Marshals. Some of these officers were obstinate, even passionate, hawks, and they did much to introduce confusion, and open conflict, into the discussions of the Special Commissions.

Of course, they also caused delay, and delay was dangerous, as events would prove. It was 6 weeks before the Special Commissions made their reports to the Conference; and even then the reports were not unanimously agreed. The debates of these "experts" reduced many keen disarmers, including Cecil, as he later recorded, to a state of consternation.

In these 6 weeks of intensive debate, morning, afternoon, and often evenings, too, the hawks produced some pearls of price.

A British War Office expert argued that whether tanks were "offensive" or "defensive" depended on the *weight* of their armour and their guns; a tank of 16 tons, he said, was obviously defensive, while tanks heavier than that might be called "offensive". By a coincidence the British Army in 1932 possessed 6 tanks of 16 tons weight—the same 6 with which they began the war against Hitler in 1939.

Adapting the British argument to suit himself, a French General maintained that a 70-ton tank must be classified as "defensive". Heavier tanks could be called "offensive". The French Army then had *one* 70-ton tank; and in 1939 they still had *one*.

In the Naval Commission, a British Admiral, Sir Dudley Pound, refused to admit that "capital ships" (battleships and armoured cruisers of large displacement tonnage) were "specifically offensive"; he maintained that they were "defensive", and, he said, "more precious than rubies to those who possess them." This British Admiralty stand on capital ships was maintained to the end of the Conference. It did more than any other single factor to delay and to confuse its work. By that time it was plain that, if capital ships had been abolished by the Conference, or if their abolition had been begun by the reduction of their number by one-third, then the same treatment could have been obtained for submarines. When war with Hitler came 6 years later, the big battleships were of singularly little value in the naval operations, while the Nazi submarine attack almost brought Britain to her knees.

This is a pretty story of the strategic foresight of Sir Dudley Pound. And also of the British naval hawks. The final comment on Sir Dudley's "rubies" speech was made when the war was over by another First Sea Lord, Admiral of the Fleet Lord Chatfield. Speaking in the House of Lords in 1954, Lord Chatfield said:

"The use of the capital ship is to destroy the enemy's capital ships. If the enemy has no capital ships, we need none either."[2]

Lord Chatfield was, perhaps, not conscious that, by this sentence, he had torpedoed his colleague Sir Dudley Pound, who had done so much to torpedo the Disarmament Conference of 1932.

Nor, perhaps, was he conscious that he was stating a particular application of the basic argument for general World Disarmament.

The Hawks struggled stubbornly in the "Special Commissions". But whatever arguments they produced to prove that their favourite weapons—tanks or battleships or bombers—were not "offensive", there were always Staff Officers from the "middle" or smaller powers to

---

2 *Hansard*, House of Lords, December 2nd, 1954, col. 139. Cecil had used this identical argument in almost the same words in his speech to the opening session of the Disarmament Conference described above. Lord Chatfield was probably unaware that Cecil had foreseen what the experience of the Second World War would prove.

answer them. I remember in particular memoranda about tanks written by the military advisers of the Dutch and the Canadian delegations. The longer the debate went on, the more completely was the general opinion of the Conference convinced that the weapons described by Cecil as "offensive" in his opening speech were, indeed, "specifically offensive", "specifically efficacious against national defence", and "most threatening to civilians".

Of course, the debates in the Naval, Land and Air Commissions had taken far longer than they should have done. Of course, the British experts' stand on tanks and battleships and bombers was alarming. The Press had given a picture to the public of disagreement and confusion. Cecil's consternation was understandable.

But in Geneva, the Reports of the Commissions, when at last they reached the Conference, were very clearly a full triumph for the thesis which Cecil had propounded on the opening day. The vast majority of the Delegations received them with enthusiasm.

CHAPTER 7

President Hoover's Disarmament Proposals, June 1932

The Reports were swiftly followed by another triumph for Cecil that was more startling still.

On June 22nd, 1932, President Herbert Hoover of the United States laid a plan[1] before the Conference for drastic world disarmament by land, sea and air. *The plan was wholly based on Cecil's principle.*

Hoover began his plan by quoting the Briand–Kellogg Pact of 1928, by which, he said, "the nations of the world have agreed that they will use their arms solely in defence. . . ."

"This reduction (of armaments) should be carried out, not only by broad general cuts in armaments, *but by increasing the comparative power of defence through decreases in the power of attack.*"

To this end, the President went on:

"In order to *reduce the offensive character of all land* forces as distinguished from their *defensive* character. . . . . . . (he proposed) *the abolition of all tanks, of all chemical warfare, and all large mobile guns.*"

The President proposed the abolition of all bombing aircraft; the prohibition by international law of all bombardment from the air; and the stringent limitation of the size and numbers of fighter aircraft.

He proposed the reduction by *one third of battleships and submarines*, and by *one quarter of aircraft carriers*, cruisers and destroyers, no nation to retain a tonnage of submarines more than 35,000 tons.

"The plan", said the President, *"would greatly reduce offensive strength compared to defensive strength, in all nations."*[2]

Thus the whole of the Hoover programme was founded on the

1 LN Document ix, Disarmament 1932 1 x 64 p. 141.
2 *Minutes of the General Commission,* Volume I, pp. 122–3.

principle of Qualitative Disarmament, and his naval proposals were avowedly intended to abolish capital ships, aircraft carriers and submarines by successive stages, of which this was to be the first.

The Hoover plan made a tremendous impact on the Conference. His chief delegate, Hugh Gibson, a career diplomat who was then Ambassador in Brussels, had told me in confidence (he was a friend with whom I used to stay in Geneva), that "something big" was coming up; the Press had heard it, too, (though not from me!); the Conference hall was packed to the doors, with the public in serried rows filling every foot of space. There was the murmuring and the agitated movement of suppressed excitement before Hugh Gibson rose. As his unemotional reading of his typewritten address unfolded the arguments and the proposals of the Hoover plan, the excitement mounted. After he had finished reading the President's plan, Mr. Gibson explained that this was no empty gesture on the part of his Government; if the Hoover proposals were accepted, the U.S. would scrap over 300,000 tons of the naval ships in the U.S. Fleet, and would give up their right under the Washington Treaty to build 50,000 tons of new ships, they would destroy more than a thousand (1,000) of their large calibre mobile guns and 900 tanks; and they would also eliminate 300 bombing aircraft. His audience agreed with Mr. Gibson that this would be a very significant measure of Disarmament by a nation of great potential military power.

Mr. Gibson further estimated that, if the President's plan were generally accepted and carried out, the world's armaments would be reduced by more than one-third. When he sat down, there was a veritable explosion of applause, clapping and cheers, from the Delegates, the Press, and—quite improperly—from the well informed spectators in the public gallery and on the floor. In spite of the rumours that had spread before his speech, he had achieved surprise and had evoked an almost turbulent support.

CHAPTER 8

The General Commission Debate on President Hoover's Proposals, June 22nd

If the delegates of all the States represented in the Conference had been allowed to follow Hugh Gibson in an immediate and continuous debate, there is no doubt that there would have been general and, perhaps, overwhelming support for the Hoover plan.

But this did not happen, because Arthur Henderson had been obliged to accept a compromise on the procedure of the Conference—a compromise which I believe he would have rejected, if he had still had the authority and influence of a Secretary of State.

Simon said in the General Commission that Henderson proposed the private talks. I cannot say from my recollection of these events that Simon's statement was untrue; but, if true, I find it surprising, and Henderson was certainly unhappy about the way the private talks were worked.

The compromise meant that the procedure of the Conference was a mixture on the one hand, of the League of Nations "parliamentary" method of open debate in public session, with the Press and unofficial observers present; and, on the other, of "private" or "secret" consultations among the representatives of some of the Great Powers—consultations like those of the old diplomacy of pre-war days! I say "among some of the Great Powers" because those who took part were the Delegates of the U.S.A., Britain, France, Italy and Japan—the Soviet Union were never invited to join in, and Litvinoff took no part in them at all; indeed, Litvinoff made it very plain that he resented this lapse into the practices of the old diplomacy, as did the Delegates of Czechoslovakia (Benes), Spain (Madariaga) and others, at various times.

This anachronistic mixture of the old and the new methods of conducting international business meant in practice that the meetings of the Conference could be suspended while the Delegates of the Great Powers (minus Russia) held what Geneva called "hotel bedroom" conversations; and it was the Bureau of the Conference, in which Great Powers influence was predominant, which decided when the suspensions should occur.

From first to last these "hotel bedroom" conversations never produced the smallest advance towards agreement on Disarmament; indeed, the delays and acrimony they caused seemed to me at the time to be one of the factors that helped to cause the final failure of the Conference.

Certainly they helped powerfully to defeat the Hoover plan.

When Hugh Gibson asked for a meeting of the General Commission at which he could read the President's message, the Great Powers—on the initiative of Simon, if I remember rightly—had been engaged for some time in "hotel bedroom" talks. The talks were proving sterile, and the suspension of their work was causing impatience, not to say defeatism and revolt among the other Delegations. It was to counteract this widespread feeling of malaise, which was reflected in the Press and among the public, that Hoover made his bold proposals. But the unhappy compromise on procedure led to a most unhappy result after Hugh Gibson's successful speech.

By some agreement in the Bureau—I never knew how it was done—Simon had persuaded Henderson that only the Delegates of the Great Powers might speak in the Session at which Gibson unveiled the President's plan. All other Delegates must wait until a later meeting, after the "hotel bedroom" talks had been concluded.

I cannot believe that Henderson willingly agreed to this arrangement; but willingly or not, as President he undertook to carry it out. There was only one deviation from what had become accepted practice—Litvinoff, not a "hotel bedroom" partner, was allowed to speak.

But Simon was the first to follow Gibson. He made a speech as long as Gibson's or longer; but it made so little impression on my mind that I have had to read the records to recall anything he said.

It was, of course, a very smooth performance. He knew he must speak words of welcome for the Hoover plan, for he knew how popular it would be with the British public: two days later he was to telegraph to his

Cabinet colleagues in London that opinion in *Geneva* made it essential that the British Government should make a public statement welcoming the plan.

So, with many well-turned phrases, he paid Hoover and Gibson compliments of various kinds. He "warmly welcomed the breadth of view" shown by Mr. Hoover; he said that "the latest contribution" of the U.S.A. to "the talk of finding common ground" would be of "the greatest possible value".

But he made no commitment to accept the plan, or any part of it; "latest contribution" indeed, was a subtle touch, which implied that the plan was like many other proposals that had been made, and not a brave attempt to bring a world Treaty into actual existence at an early date. Before he ended, Simon had given a plain hint that he would put forward alternative proposals—a hint which became a concrete reality, and a reality which destroyed the Hoover plan. Simon had shown no enthusiasm for the plan, and he roused no enthusiasm among his audience—there was, indeed, resentment against the substance and the tone of what he said.

Simon was followed by the Delegate of France—no longer Tardien, who, with his Right-wing colleagues, had fallen from power in a General Election. His successor as Minister for War and delegate to the Geneva Conference was Jean Paul-Boncour, a strong supporter of the League and of Disarmament.

His welcome to the Hoover plan was warmer than Simon's; he said in the first paragraph of his speech that it was a matter for congratulation that the President's proposals would "give a new impetus to the Conference and stimulate its determination to achieve success".

He said a little later: "while sincerely supporting the proposals"—and when Paul-Boncour said "sincerely" he meant it.

But for the rest of what he said, it was, no doubt inevitably, a repetition in several difficult contexts and several different forms, of the constant French theme, urged by French Governments both of Right and Left for 15 years—the theme that: "in accordance with the spirit of the Covenant and its very precise wording, the reduction of armaments was bound up with the organisation of international security".

Paul-Boncour was right, of course, The Covenant, and Cecil's Treaty of Mutual Assistance of 1933, and the Geneva Protocol of 1924, were the formal recognition by many Governments and by eminent British statesmen (Robert Cecil, Arthur Henderson, J. Ramsay MacDonald) that he was right.

And of course Sir Maurice Hankey and the other British hawks were entirely wrong to say that the Covenant was obscure, and most ludicrously wrong to argue that "the organisation of international security" through the League would have meant an additional "military commitment" which, with our imperial and Locarno obligations, Britain could not afford to make. The reverse was obviously true—once we had accepted the Locarno obligation to support either France or Germany, whichever might be attacked by the other, "the organisation of international security" would bring us other, sorely needed allies—the Second World War was to show how sorely needed—and it would thus *lighten* the burden of our military commitments.

But while the British hawks made a glaring strategical mistake in rejecting the obligations of the Covenant, and in trying to weaken them, so the French, hawks and internationalists alike, made a vast political mistake in denigrating the value of the Covenant sanctions, and in demanding military guarantees from other states for French "security". However sound their argument, they used the word "security" so often that people in Geneva simply ceased to listen when they heard it. Thus Paul-Boncur's honest welcome for the Hoover plan made less impact on his audience that it should have done.

Not only so. Within a year events in the Conference and in Europe were to show that the Delegate of France would have done far better to accept the Hoover plan without conditions, and to strive with all his power for its acceptance. For if it had come into force, Germany would have remained totally disarmed in fulfilment of the Treaty of Versailles; Hitler would have been disarmed; France would have been disarmed, but she would have been *safe*; she would have been spared the humiliations and and the sufferings of the Second World War.

After Boncour came Litvinoff, the only speaker in this session who was not taking part in the "hotel-Bedroom" talks.

Hugh Gibson had been nervous about Russia.

Before his first arrival in 1928, Litvinoff had been Soviet Foreign Minister for 7 years. But he had stayed in Moscow; hardly anybody knew him; he seemed like a dim, mysterious, and perhaps, a dangerous being from another world.

But on his first morning in Geneva in 1928, a trivial episode had gone far to create the feeling that, after all, he might be human.

He had an Irish wife, whose Christian name was Ivy; in 1928 she was well-advanced in middle age. As she came out with Litvinoff from the first session of the Preparatory Disarmament Commission, she found herself almost jostling the British Delegate, Cecil's successor, a Tory Irish Lord of large proportions, who rejoiced in the title of Lord Cushendun of Cushendun.

To his amazement, and to the joy of the delegates who were crowded round, Mrs. Litvinoff took the British Delegate, the ageing Tory Lord, by the arms, and said in an ingratiating tone: "Oh, Lord Cushendun, I'm so glad to see you again. Do you remember? My name's Ivy. Last time we met I sat on your knee and you fed me chocolates."

Geneva was enchanted by the story, and barriers seemed to fall away between the League community and these alien Muscovites.

But in June, 1932, what was Litvinoff going to say? By this time he was personally well-known, and well-respected (in a book written a little later, Cecil, the aristocrat and anti-Communist, called Litvinoff a sound colleague).

But what would Litvinoff say? Russia was not yet a Member of the League; for 4 years, in the Preparatory Commission, Litvinoff had been preaching general and complete disarmament. What would he say in answer to Hoover's plan?

To the immense relief of the Conference, and of Henderson, there came no blustering propaganda. In a quiet speech, he began, indeed, by chiding the Conference for its lack of progress. But he did so in a tone of conciliatory common sense. When he reached the Hoover plan, he welcomed the proposals because, in some respects, they adopted the Soviet proposals which he had made. But in other respects they would need further consideration. They did not definitely and forever end the arms race. They did not give equality to all the prospective signatory Powers (Germany and her First War Allies).

But he ended with these words, as officially recorded by the League stenographers:

He would propose that the discussion (of the Hoover plan) be not too long postponed, (this followed a polite complaint about the "private" talks which Hugh Gibson had interrupted) so that *the Delegations might have an early opportunity to express at least their attitude in principle towards the proposals* of the President of the United States. *In this way he hoped the work of the Conference would really begin.*

Litvinoff's hearers judged this to be a cordial welcome to the U.S. Plan, and concluded that Russia would certainly sign the Treaty which Hoover proposed.

So Litvinoff sat down to sighs of heartfelt relief, grunts of satisfaction, and also—and notably—to waves of restrained, but all the same quite warm applause.

Another triumph for Hoover came at once.

Nadolny was not an exciting orator. But what he might say for Germany was of supreme importance. Had Hoover gone far enough to meet the claims of the Government of the Weimar Republic; and to still or to defeat the rancour taunts of Hitler? What Nadolny would say was awaited with bated breath by those who understood the international situation and the precarious hold on power of his democratic masters in Berlin.

Nadolny surpassed Hugh Gibson's highest hopes.

In his opening sentence, he said that: "The German delegation had taken cognizance of President Hoover's proposals *with keen interest and special satisfaction.* He thought that the Conference must necessarily be glad that this fresh initiative had been taken" . . . . . Mr. Nadolny went on: *"The very judicious proposals which Mr. Gibson had submitted would,* Mr. Nadolny sincerely hoped, *give the Conference a fresh stimulus and facilitate its work.*

Mr. Nadolny warmly approved the principle on which President Hoover's message was based . . . . . "No better way could be imagined of achieving that very security which all states were rightly demanding and which was promised to them all in Article 8 of the Covenant."

Mr. Nadolny expressed his hope that the Conference would agree on Disarmament measures going even further than the President proposed, since this would help to solve the problem of "legal equality" for Germany and her ex-allies, such equality, the establishment of which was one of the essential conditions for the Conference's ultimate success.

But he ended by saying again that *"the German Delegation welcomed with warmest sympathy the very important declaration of the United States Delegation.''*

This concluding sentence and the other favourable words quoted above, left the delegates in no doubt that the Weimar Republic, in spite of Nadolny's words about "legal equality" would sign and carry out a world disarmament treaty on the basis which the U.S. President proposed.

The speeches of Litvinoff and Nadolny were judged by the Delegates in the General Commission, and by the Press and public, to be little short of a notable victory for President Hoover and his ambitious plan.

Something even better, and something quite unexpected, was to follow.

The next in this first, restricted day's debate was Signor Grandi, the Foreign Minister of Italy.

Grandi was a Fascist, or he would not have been there. But he was a Fascist with a difference.

He had first come to Geneva 8 or 9 years before, when he held the office of Under-Secretary for Foreign Affairs. The memory of Mussolini's defeat by the League Assembly over Corfu in 1923 was then still fresh in the mind of every Delegation to the Council and Assembly. Italy was still almost a pariah, nation, and the word "Fascist" was anathema. Grandi set himself to restore Italy's good name by quiet, but consistent and constructive support for the League and all its works.

He soon created a strong personal situation in Geneva, where people of widely different political opinions came to like and trust him.

His policy was no less popular in Italy, and both Press and public gave him their openly expressed approval. As his stature grew in League circles and at home, Mussolini, although still an enemy of the League, found it advisable, or necessary, to make him Foreign Minister.

But no one in Geneva believed that the two men were really in agreement over foreign policy, and least of all over armaments. Mussolini had never concealed his hope that he could make Fascist Italy "great" by force of arms; as the Conference of 1932 approached, Grandi showed himself more and more favourable to Disarmament. By 1932, many people were saying that Grandi was becoming almost a declared rival to Mussolini, and that if the Conference succeeded, he would use that success to drive Mussolini from power, and to rule Italy himself instead.

Certainly this theory was borne out by the speech which Grandi made on this afternoon of June 22nd.

He had taken immense trouble over its preparation. To the amazement of the General Commission, he spoke, for the first time in his life, in *English*. And it was not stumbling, English, ill-spoken, ill-pronounced and difficult to understand. On the contrary, it was fluent, accurately pronounced, and fully understood by every hearer. Whether he had had a long series of English lessons was a matter of speculation; certain it was that his speech had been repeatedly and meticulously rehearsed.

But the substance of his speech was no less of a surprise to the General Commission than the language in which it was delivered.

In the first paragraph of his speech, Grandi said that he had been able to communicate Hoover's plan to Mussolini, and as a result could make the following statement:

"Italy accepts entirely and in all its parts the Disarmament plan just submitted to the General Commission by the United States Delegation".

This was gall and wormwood to Mussolini, as events were soon to show, and especially the introductory words about consultation with "the head of his Government". The Duke had only accepted them because opinion in Italy compelled him to.

But it was a resounding victory for Grandi, and for Hoover.

Grandi proceeded to rub in the importance of his opening paragraph by reciting in detail all the reductions of armed forces and abolitions of "offensive" weapons that Hoover proposed, from "the abolition of heavy mobile artillery to the abolition of chemical and biological warfare".

Grandi said that he would not add other words to what he had said "he desired by this simple list to emphasise how complete was Italy's adhesion. Italy was a country armed on land, on sea and in the air and by accepting the U.S. proposal she was prepared to make substantial and well defined sacrifices. She would, however, make them willingly because she was deeply convinced that a peaceful Commonwealth of nations could only be based on the sacrifices that every country should and would be willing to make".

And he further expressed the hope that "all the nations represented at the Conference would respond to that (the Presidents) appeal to common sense and good will".

Grandi sat down to an ovation from delegations, press, and most improperly from the public. There was a general feeling that his speech would have been an admirable climax to the afternoon's discussion which Hugh Gibson had begun.

But there was one more speaker. In order to challenge the claim that the day's debate should be confined to great power delegates who were taking part in the "hotel bedroom" talks, Senor Salvador de Madariaga had insisted that he must make a Spanish contribution to the opening round of speeches about the Hoover plan.

His key sentence was this:

"Needless to say, Spain was ready to approve the U.S. claim entirely; Subject to discussion of details."

This was what the General Commission wanted to hear. But Madariaga went on to say that on certain points his Government would like to go beyond the U.S. President's proposals. They would have welcomed:

(i)   the total abolition of all military aviation;
(ii) international control of the manufacture of and trade in arms
(iii) the more constructive oorganization of peace, meaning the acceptance of the thesis is constantly put forward by the French.

The majority of the General Commission agreed with Madariaga on his first two points, and several agreed with his third. But they were not sure that the Hugh Gibson debate was the right time to bring them forward. They did not want the best to be the enemy of the good and it was the Spanish endorsement of Hugh Gibson's statement that they welcomed.

When Madariaga sat down, Henderson made a speech in which he repeated his hope that "the conversations could be terminated with all possible speed". He said "there were a very large number of other delegates waiting at Geneva who came to him—as indeed those heads of delegations had done the day before, to ask what the situation was and as he was not permitted to take part in these conversations, he was not in a position to inform his colleagues". On this restless, not to say impatient note, the General Commission adjourned and it did not meet till July 7th—a gap of 15 days.

CHAPTER 9

The General Commission Debate on the Hoover Plan—July 7th and 8th, 1932

During the fortnight's interval since the Hoover Plan was laid before the General Commission the 'hotel bedroom' talks continued, and the delegates of many other nations went back to their respective capitals to consult their Governments. Simon sent a telegram to the British Cabinet saying that opinion in Geneva demanded a statement by Britain that Britain welcomed the Hoover Plan.

But shortly after he sent this telegram, Simon returned himself to London, abandoning the private conversations and engaged on very different work.

On July 7th he made a statement in the House of Commons which was simultaneously circulated to all delegations at Geneva. This statement and its disastrous effect on the Conference will be dealt with in the next chapter. But Simon's statement did not prevent the continuation of the Debate on the Hoover Plan in the General Commission. This debate took place in the afternoon of July 7th and in two sessions in the morning and afternoon of July 8th.

There were speeches from delegates of 30 other nations and every single speech welcomed the Hoover Plan, and almost every delegate who spoke committed his Government to its full acceptance and execution. Some two or three delegations, Yugoslavia among them, said that they would also like to see the Conference accept the French proposals about security. But none who said this suggested that his Government would refuse to sign a Hoover Treaty if the French proposals were not added.

Here are some extracts from the debates in the three sittings of the General Commission:

Monsieur Dupré of Canada said that "a substantial reduction of military budgets would make so much capital available for productive purposes and social work that no-one could give a moments thought to it without desiring it. Nothing would be better calculated to revive business and confidence—the barometer of the business world".

Monsieur Dupré was speaking in the later stages of the Great World Slump at the beginning of the 1930s. His worlds apply with force to the situation of 1978.

Monsieur Dupré further said "the Canadian Delegation was therefore anxious that all the delegations should agree to embark upon and persevere in the course indicated by the President of the United States" and "the time had come to make a supreme effort. Let them, therefore, make it with all the power and dis-interestedness of which they were capable, remembering in that grave and epoch-making hour the Almighty's message: "Peace on earth to men of good will".

Count Carton de Wiart of Belgium said that "President Hoover's initiative had made a profound impression in his country". Quoting President Hoover "the folly" of "breaking its back over military expenditure" and expressing his Government's full agreement with the principle of the U.S. plan, he said "on all those points the Belgian delegation was in complete agreement with President Hoover". He thought that "if before closing the first stage of its work, the Conference was able . . . . . to state that an agreement had been reached as to those prohibitions (i.e. President Hoover's proposal to abolish offensive weapons) it would have satisfied the immediate desire of public opinion, that tangible and concrete results should come from its laborious deliberations."

Monsieur de Macedo Soares of Brazil "wished first to express his great satisfaction at the attitude adopted by the President of the United States, who had affirmed in concrete terms the high-minded view of the American people, with regard to the thesis previously formulated by President Wilson . . . the abolition of secret diplomacy". Further, "the Brazilian Delegation enthusiastically welcomed President Hoover's magnificent gesture by which the U.S. Government's instructions to its delegates at the Conference had been made public. The Brazilian delegation was convinced that, within the framework of President Hoover's instructions, the Conference could, in its first stage, find solutions for all the problems of disarmament, and it would therefore urge that his proposals be discussed immediately".

Cemal Husnu Bey of Turkey said that "his delegation had welcomed President Hoover's proposal with the warmest sympathy. The suggestions contained in them represented a real and bold step towards the ideal of which the achievement was awaited by world public opinion with a legitimate impatience that was steadily gathering force. The principles which . . . . . should guide the nations on the road to disarmament were in complete harmony with those upheld by the Turkish delegation since the beginning of the Conference's work".

Monsieur de Agurro y Bethancourt of Cuba said that "the Government of Cuba desired entirely to associate itself with the proposals made by the U.S. delegation . . . . . and earnestly hoped that those proposals would be accepted in their entirety or as far as possible".

Herr Pflug of Austria raised the question of the legal equality under Article 8 of the Covenant, of states disarmed by the Treaties of Peace of 1919; but he also said that "the Austrian delegation was glad to associate itself with the principles of reduction proposed" by the United States.

Mr. Irgens of Norway said that "the Norwegian delegation not only approved the principles underlying the important declaration read by the U.S. Delegation, but that it also accepted the main lines of that proposal. Its acceptance was especially cordial as the plan briefly described in President Hoover's message would involve on the one hand considerable reduction in expenditure on armaments, and on the other hand would largely eliminate military, naval and air factors which exposed the states to the possibility of sudden attack."

"The Norwegian delegate ended his speech by paying a tribute to President Hoover 'who had stimulated in no small degree the work of the Conference, and expressed the hope that the General Commission would, before closing, arrive at definite conclusions and undertakings' ".

Mr. Deschamps of the Dominican Republic said that his Government "adhered with the utmost sincerity and without any reservations, to the proposal of Mr. Hoover," . . . . . "the people of the Dominican Republic ardently desired peace for Europe, the only source and centre of Western civilisation—indeed, it would be no exaggeration to say of modern civilisation, throughout the world. . . . . . The Dominican Republic, inspired by a high sense of human solidarity . . . . . gave their cooperation to the compulsory decrease of attacking forces." He said President Hoover had "earned the gratitude of all mankind".

Mr. Erich of Finland expressed "an absolute preference for defensive armaments was to strengthen the security of the nations . . . . . and was prepared to accept the U.S. Proposals." He said, however, that the proposal must be applied with "a certain elasticity" to take account of the position of the smaller nations.

Mr. de Masirevich of Hungary stated that the Hungarian delegation "readily accepted and earnestly wished to give all the support in its power to the general purpose of the initiative" of the U.S., "because it would promote the reduction of arms" and "the equal rights to all nations on the basis of Article 8 of the Covenant". This purpose "was not interfered with by the President's message".

Mr. Echou of Denmark expressed "sincere sympathy with the proposal and warmly supported President Hoover's proposal. . . . . . The Danish delegation was in complete agreement with the ideas embodied in the U.S. Proposal and would consequently be very glad to co-operate, as far as lay in its power".

Thus, in this second sitting on the Hoover plan, speeches were made by the delegations of 11 countries without one word of opposition to

what the President proposed and with only a single hesitant asser-
tion that the French demand for the International Organisation of
Security must also be accepted.

In the Third sitting on the Hoover plan, *Mr. Castillo Najera of Mexico*
spoke first. He said "President Hoover's message had come as a ray
of hope to lighten the darkness, and was a happy augury of the
fulfilment of their ardent desire." Further "the Mexican delegation
warmly acclaimed President Hoover's proposal . . . . . The pacific
intentions clearly revealed by the Hoover proposal would doubtless
help to facilitate international co-operation between all the nations
of the world".
This declaration from Mexico whose disputes with the United
States had been frequent and acute, was of notable importance.

Mr. Lo of China said that China was "ready to accept that scheme"
(outlined in the U.S. proposal). Mr. Lo also raised the question of
the manufacture of an international trade in arms. At that time
Western supplies of arms to Chinese war lords were helping to ferment
a long period of disastrous civil wars.

Mr. Sandler of Sweden who was shortly to become Foreign Minister in
a new Social Democratic Government which held power for many
years, said on behalf of his country "that he hoped that the Conference would respond by acts to the appeal of the United States of
America, in the spirit which inspired President Hoover to begin his
proposal with the words: 'The time has come'.".

General Laidoner of Estonia said that President Hoover's message
"had aroused the very greatest interest in all countries and his
proposals had been, and were being, very carefully examined" . . . . .
and "hoped that the Conference would come to a general agreement" on qualitative disarmament. He ended by hoping that "the
combined efforts of all the delegations would enable the Conference
shortly to achieve practical results".

The next speaker was *Mr. Motta of Switzerland* who had been President of the Swiss Confederation and who had played a brilliant part

in many sessions of the League of Nations Assembly. He said: "the Swiss delegation accepted the President's proposals unconditionally and without reservations of any kind" and later said "the Swiss Delegation welcomed, not only with sympathy but with confident and sincere enthusiasm, the proposals of the President of the United States". . . . . "The chief merit of the action taken by the President was that he had brought ideas down from the abstract realm above into the world of realities".

Sir Thomas Wilford of New Zealand thanked the President for his well timed proposals for disarmament. Referring to possible alternative proposals by the British Delegation and expressing the hope that a compromise could be found, Sir Thomas ended by saying "let it get to work, for a tired and troubled world was praying for decisions."

Mr. Antoniade of Roumania said that his delegation "highly appreciated the object of the message from the President". Like all others present at the Conference they had begun a detailed study of the proposals and might find it necessary "to suggest the necessary corrections required by Article 8 of the Covenant, that being the basis of the whole of the Conference's work for disarmament."

Mr. Ansari of Persia said "the entire world had welcomed with joy President Hoover's magnificent gesture on behalf of disarmament", but the Great Powers must apply the principles which the President had expounded. He hoped they would set an example to the world.

Mr. Escalante of Venezuela said that "the U.S. proposals were an example worthy to be followed by the other countries; they at the same time, provided an important starting-point for the success of the great work of universal pacification which the present Conference was attempting to carry out for the first time in history." And that the proposals were "in accord with the interests of the small countries which were in a disadvantageous position from the point of view of defensive armaments. The Venezuelan delegation therefore warmly welcomed them and entirely accepted them in regard to land as well as air and sea forces"

Mr. Bosch of the Argentine said "the Presidents scheme represented a great and *decisive* effort to further the work of the Conference". He hoped that "a common ground could be found on which it would be able to accomplish the great results that were so fervently desired. Difficulties, no doubt, would have to be overcome, but the good will and conciliatory spirit that prevailed in the Conference would smooth them away".

Ten more speeches; only Rumania had suggested any doubt about the Hoover Plan, and the Rumanian doubt was certainly far short of opposition.

The Last Session's Debate on the Hoover Plan

In two sittings of the General Commission there had been 21 speeches with general support, indeed enthusiastic support, for what the United States' President had proposed. The last session was to continue this chorus of consent.

Mr. Rutgers of the Netherlands opened this last sitting with the following words: "The Netherlands delegation assented to President Hoover's proposals. His acceptance covered both the whole and every part of that document".

He said that the Conference must go beyond mere verbal acceptance of the President's plan; it must satisfy American opinion by something more concrete. He quoted Mr. Sandler of Sweden: "the Conference must *act*", but he added an urgent plea that on one matter the Hoover plan should be improved, aerial warfare must be made impossible: "complete abolition (of national air forces) was required".

Mr. Rutgers' speech made a strong impression on the General Commission by reason of his personal authority and of the great part which the Netherlands had always played in world affairs.

Colonel Lanskoronskis of Lithuania was "glad to be able to announce Lithuania's complete acceptance of the proposals under discussion."

Husein Aziz Khan of Afghanistan stated that the Afghan delegation "were in favour of the qualitative reduction of armaments to the

lowest possible level, and within this limit, it fully supported the
United States proposal". He also expressed readiness to co-operate
in any efforts and to support any proposals that might prove benefi-
cial and effective".

Mr. Restrepo of Colombia supported President Hoover's bold plan as
"the South Americans loved peace and thus loved the great countries which sought to establish it in the world . . . . . The Colombian
delegation would support President Hoover's proposals, so long as
no more radical proposals were advanced".

Mr. Feldmans of Latvia said that his delegation was glad, "on behalf
of the Latvian Government, to give its complete adhesion to President Hoover's generous proposal." He felt that the "proposal
offered a really universal and constructive plan" . . . . . and "as a
whole was of capital importance".

Mr. de Quevedo of Portugal "felt that the American message should be
discussed with the other proposals submitted to the Conference . . . .
in that spirit, the Portuguese delegation was glad to support the
general provisions of President Hoover's proposal, which it
regarded as a generous gesture on behalf of the common cause of
disarmament".

Mr. Costa du Rels of Bolivia said that he "supported the happy
initiative of the President of the United States . . . . . and was
prepared most cordially to support the proposal".

Mr. Mikoff of Bulgaria "welcomed sympathetically the principles on
which President Hoover's proposals were based, while reserving his
Government's right to state its views if necessary on certain aspects
of the proposed plan, particularly with regard to the relativity
which must be introduced in order to meet the special conditions of
each country.

Mr. Choumenkovich of Yugoslavia said the Yugoslav delegation
"desired to support the other delegations who, from the platform,

had paid a tribute to the Hoover plan. He said, however, that the plan should be studied together with other plans submitted, particularly the French plan relating to the positive organisation of peace".

In addition to the declarations made during the general discussion on the proposals of the President of the United States of America, the delegations of Albania, Costa Rica and Luxemburg notified the Conference of their adhesion to the proposals in the following terms:

(a) Letter from the Albanian Delegation dated July 7th, 1932 "I have the honour to inform your Excellency that the delegation to the Kingdom of Albania gives its support to the proposals made by Mr. Hoover. Will you be so kind as to communicate the above to the delegations to the Conference for the Reduction and Limitation of Armaments?. . . . ."

(Signed) Lec Kurti, Delegate of Albania.

(b) Letter from the Delegation of Costa Rica dated July 7th, 1932 "I have the honour to inform you that the Costa Rican delegation gives its full and entire support without any reservation to the proposals made by President Hoover".

(Signed) Viriato Figueredo-Lora, Delegate of Costa Rica.

(c) Letter from the Delegation of Luxemburg dated July 9th, 1932. "Having been prevented from being present at the meetings of the General commission last Thursday and Friday, I have the honour to request you to let it be known that, as the Grand-Duchy of Luxemburg has no military, naval or airforces, it is in favour of any proposal aiming at the reduction and limitation of armaments, and it therefore accedes without reservation to the American proposals".

(Signed) Ch. G. Vermaire, Substitute Delegate.

Mr. Hugh Gibson later expressed the great satisfaction which he felt as he reflected on all the speeches made about his President's plan. He claimed that 34 nations—more than two-thirds of the states taking part in the Conference—had given their warm support to the U.S. proposals.

This claim was fully justified, indeed in the atmosphere of the Conference hall itself it was difficult not to feel that the overwhelming majority of the delegates wanted the President's plan to succeed and believed that the Conference should adopt and act on it without delay.

CHAPTER 10

How Simon killed the Hoover plan

The thirty speeches made on July 7th and 8th, 1932, in this deferred debate on the Hoover Plan, and the three letters from the Governments of Costa Rica, Albania and Luxemburg, were manna to people in the League—I was one of them—who had worked and hoped for this hour for 12 years or more. Visions of a world without war grew vivid in their minds—a world freed from the squalid degradation of militarism, of Chauvenist distrust and dishonest propaganda, of the huge waste of resources needed for social betterment, but given to preparing war instead.

But their hope was muted by the thought that the Hoover Plan could only demilitarize the world, if Britain gave it her full support.

They had had good reason to expect that that support would be readily, indeed enthusiastically, given. Sir John Simon had been the prophet of Qualitative Disarmament. He had got the Conference to accept the principle. He had secured the Special Commissions' Reports. Only a month before he had vigorously defended Qualitative Disarmament in the House of Commons. Hoping to silence the hostile criticism of House of Commons' hawks, he had argued:

"There are certain weapons mentioned in Part V of the Treaty of Versailles which are prohibited to Germany, and there are certain other weapons which Germany is permitted to have. Will anybody who thinks that Qualitative Disarmament is all nonsense be good enough to tell me why the Allied and Associated Powers selected those partial weapons and prohibited Germany from having them? The answer is written on the face of the Treaty of Versailles, and it is that those weapons were then regarded as weapons which would have enabled Germany, had she been so minded, to undertake operations of offence".[1]

This was strong talk from Sir John Simon, and to anyone who believed that the purpose of armaments is national defence, what he said made an unanswerable case for the Qualitative Disarmament which he urged.

But unfortunately the militarist Members of the House whom he was trying to convert showed no interest in the logic of his argument about national defence. They were not only immovably convinced that Qualitative Disarmament was "nonsense"; they believed that *all* Disarmament was nonsense; that armaments are a good thing in themselves; that the more armaments a nation had, the safer and the *greater* it would be; they believed in the value of military power with more conviction than they believed in aything else.

Of course, Members of the House were, in principle, supporters of the League. Still others, among them Winston Churchill, were deeply disturbed when Simon faced them with what had then become the brutal truth:

"We have to choose, and our choice is very clear. Shall we disarm ourselves, or shall we allow the Germans to re-arm?"[2]

Simon did Simon's best, in the House of Commons and elsewhere. But it was not good enough. And he did not understand the great strength he could command if he stood in Britain for the policy he had preached in the Conference in Geneva.

There were more than 500 Tories in the House of Commons, and the great majority were hostile to Disarmament and the League. But the people who had sent them to the House, the electors, took a very different view. As events were soon to show, they were very strongly *for* Disarmament.[3]

If Simon, and his Parliamentary Secretary, Anthony Eden, who shared Simon's view, had stood firm for Qualitative Disarmament and for the Hoover Plan, and if they had threatened to resign unless they got their way, they would have rallied such widespread popular support that the Government and the Parliamentary hawks would have had no option but to submit.

1   *Hansard,* House of Commons, May 13th, 1932, col. 2334.
2   *Hansard,* House of Commons, May 13th 1932.
3   See pp. 136–9.

But Simon had no thought of resignation. And he had opposition in the "National" Cabinet, as well as in the House.

The First Lord of the Admiralty was a certain Eyres-Monsell, a Naval Officer (retired). His only political ambition was to keep as many British warships on the oceans as he could—never mind what other nations had. In the early weeks of the Disarmament Conference, he had come to Geneva for a few days, had sat in a few sessions in restless silence, and on the evening when he left again for London, he had said to a group of members of the British Delegation: "The sooner your bloody conference is wound up, the better for all concerned". I happened to be in the lobby of the Hotel Beau Rivage when he said it, and I heard him speak the words.

Douglas Hogg, already the first Lord Hailsham, was Secretary of State for War. He was as obstinately in favour of keeping tanks and heavy mobile guns as Eyres-Monsell was in favour of keeping battleships and aircraft carriers.

Lord Londonderry was the Secretary of State for Air. In 1935, speaking in the House of Lords about the events of 1932, he made his most famous ever speech:

"I had the greatest difficulty, amid the public outcry, [Cecil's Disarmament Campaign] in saving the bomber."

These men were all bitterly hostile to Simon's Qualitative Disarmament. They were died-in-the-wool hawks, and they had the sympathy of other right-wing Ministers in the Cabinet; even ex-Liberals like Herbert Samuel seemed to waver about tanks.

Simon had become obsessed by this opposition before the Hoover plan was launched. He realized that, so far as the House and the Cabinet were concerned, his speech on May 13th had definitely failed.

He understood—he had clearly told the House—that, if the Geneva Conference did not disarm the world, then Germany would inevitably re-arm. He knew that, with the rising power of Hitler, this would be dangerous in the extreme. But the danger to Simon from the British hawks seemed of even greater and more urgent import. At all costs, Simon must remain the Secretary of State for Foreign Affairs.

So what could Simon say about the Hoover Plan in that Geneva meeting on June 22nd in which such vast world issues were at stake?

He had definitely decided that he could not make the speech of warm endorsement for which so many of his audience hoped.

So he made the speech which has been summarized in chapter 8 above—an empty compliment about the President's "breadth of view"; non-committal platitudes about the need for compromise and mutual-concessions—perhaps a hint that some parts of Hoover's plan would be rejected; concluding paragraphs on Naval armaments, which hinted more clearly that Britain would put alternative proposals before the Conference. And some words which roused the indignation of the U.S. Delegates—the British proposals would mean "more Disarmament" by measures which would be more "adequate" and more "appropriate".

No one had thought this speech was very promising. But it did not prepare them for the British counter-plan which Simon launched by a statement in the House of Commons on July 7th, with distribution of the text that same evening to the Delegations in Geneva.

The counter-plan proved to be a flat rejection of almost everything that Hoover had proposed.

1. It argued at length that Britain could make no further reduction in the manpower of her Forces. Indeed, their strength was already less than that which the President's principles would allow. This passage of the statement was unwelcome to the U.S. Delegation. The British argument might be a precedent which other Governments would adopt.

2. It proposed "the abolition of all mobile guns of a calibre greater than 155 mm (6.1 inch calibre)". The U.S. had proposed all guns over 105 mm (4.1 inch). The difference in explosive power was great; the offensive power of 6.1 inch guns very considerable.

3. It proposed "the abolition of all tanks above a weight of 20 tons". It agreed that tanks above that weight "are especially suitable for offensive employment in battle". But tanks of less than 20 tons not only save human life, but also enable the number of effectives in a land army to be reduced. To forbid them would thus defeat one of the purposes of Disarmament.

4. The statement proposed the prohibition of bombing from the air, "save within limits to be laid down as precisely as possible in an international convention". This meant that Britain must be free to "police" the North West Frontier of India and Iraq by bombing; therefore the Disarmament Treaty must permit the retention of bombing

aircraft, and must allow Britain to train her Air Force pilots in the technique of bombing.

This part of the British statement caused acute resentment among other Delegations in the Conference.

5. The statement proposed "a strict limitation in the unladen weight of all military and naval aircraft"—but with the exception of "troop carriers and flying boats", the size of which was to be unrestricted.

6. It proposed "a restriction in the numbers of all military and naval aircraft"—but no figure was named.

7. The statement added a sermon about Britain's dependence on aircraft for the fulfilment of her "mandatory duties" in her Colonial possessions—a sermon which also pointed out that Britain had only the fifth largest fleet of military and naval aircraft.

8. But it was on Naval armaments that the British statement diverged most widely from the Hoover Plan.

It rejected altogether the reduction in the numbers of battleships, aircraft carriers and submarines which the President had proposed, and entirely disregarded his obvious intention that these classes of warships should be wholly abolished by successive stages, so that legal equality with Germany in respect of navies might in due course be reached.

It proposed instead that all existing British warships should be retained, but that when their useful life ended in 1937, the battleships should be replaced by much smaller vessels, carrying less powerful guns. The new limits proposed were 22,000 tons displacement, and 11-inch guns, instead of the Washington Naval Treaty limits of 35,000 tons and 16-inch guns.

9. The statement similarly proposed that future aircraft carriers should be reduced from the Washington limit of 27,000 tons and 8-inch guns to 22,000 tons and 6.1-inch guns.

10. It proposed the reduction of future cruisers to 7000 tons, with 6.1-inch guns.

11. It proposed the total abolition of submarines, or failing that, the limitation of the size of submarines to 250 tons displacement.

The statement argues that these proposals would mean a greater total reduction of naval tonnage, and therefore of the cost of navies, than the Hoover Plan.

But:

1. These naval proposals left unmentioned the fact that it involved the retention of classes of weapons which Germany was forbidden to have. Germany was sure to reject any treaty based on these proposals, unless she were given the right to build such vessels too.

2. The proposed reduction in the size of battleships and aircraft carriers reflected the views of a strong body of naval experts, led by Admiral Richmond, who urged that the existing vessels were far too large, and far too vulnerable to submarine and aircraft attack. Experience in the Second World War proved that this school was right. The Conference regarded the British proposal, not as one for Disarmament, but as a proposal to increase the fighting strength of the British Navy.

3. Everybody knew that the British proposal to abolish submarines would never be accepted by other naval powers, unless battleships were abolished, too. Hoover's proposal could have led to the elimination of both classes of warships within a short period of time. But while they planned to keep their battle fleet, it was more propaganda.

4. The British proposal about cruisers was particularly unwelcome to the U.S. Delegates. The U.S. and British Naval experts had clashed on the subject at the Coolidge Conference. The Americans had constantly asserted there that they needed ships of 10,000 tons, because they had no naval bases, whereas the British had bases in every corner of the globe, and, could, therefore, do with smaller ships. The dispute had led to harsh feelings in 1927; the new proposal in 1932 rubbed an old and unhealed wound.

For Simon to say, as he did, that the proposals in his Statement of July 7th meant more Disarmament than the Hoover Plan, was to add insult to injury.

Hoover had sought to effect a large and quick reduction of world armaments. He had done so by proposing the abolition by all nations of almost all the weapons of attack, the offensive weapons, which Germany had been forbidden to possess. He had done so in such a way that there was an excellent chance that Germany would consent to remain bound by the Treaty of Versailles.

Simon proposed in his statement that all nations (presumably except Germany) should be free to retain mobile guns of larger calibre than Germany was allowed to possess, and to retain tanks and military and naval aircraft and battleships and aircraft carriers.

This programme thwarted the whole purpose of the Hoover Plan, which was to strengthen the national defence of every nation by the general abolition of the weapons of offence.

There was no chance that Germany would accept a Treaty on such terms as these, and Simon had told the House of Commons that the other nations had to choose: they must disarm themselves or allow Germany to re-arm. And everybody knew already in July 1932 that, if Germany re-armed, it would be Hitler who did it, and that that, almost certainly, would mean another war.

It was with this prospect in his mind that Simon surrendered to the Cabinet hawks. He decided that he must kill the Hoover Plan rather than risk his tenure of the Foreign Office.

Of course, this tragic sequence of events need not have happened, if Hoover had understood how the machinery of a League Conference could be used.

The contemporary authors of the *Survey of International Affairs* published by the British Royal Institute of International Affairs in 1933, made the following comment:

> "The circulation of the British proposals at this moment made an unfortunate impression, since it appeared to be an attempt to diminish the effect of the small Powers' chorus of approval of the Hoover plan".[4]

Of course, the fortnight's break had in itself done something to cool the atmosphere of enthusiasm which had been generated on June 22nd.

But the ardent feeling of that day could have been re-kindled.

There were still lots of Delegates who would try to save the Conference, and who would go on fighting for the principle which Hoover, following Cecil and Simon himself, had so dramatically declared.

There were some, like me, who felt that if the President had sent his Secretary of War, Mr. Newton D. Baker, to represent him in the Conference, all might have been saved. Cecil—and others, not least Briand and Austen Chamberlain—had proved in the League of Nations that public parliamentary debate could achieve most notable results. If Mr. Newton D. Baker, a tough and eloquent debater, had been there, he could have

4 *Survey of International Affairs*, 1932, p. 247.

pulverized the British counter-plan. If he had taken Simon limb from limb, and declared the President's resolute intention to press his plan, Mr. Baker might have roused the sympathetic Baldwin from his lethargy, and he would have roused the British people to most active support. If he had enlarged on the duty of Members of the League to carry out the binding, legal obligations of Article 8 of the Covenant, and of Part V of the Treaty of Versailles, that, coming from the spokesman of the United States, would have hit the British hard—they still took pride in the fact that, unlike the Kaiser's Germany, they faithfully observed the Treaties they had signed. Mr. Baker could have embroidered Simon's fateful choice—"shall we disarm, or shall Germany re-arm?" He could have shown that the choice was real and urgent—if the Conference was allowed to fail, Germany would certainly re-arm. He could have roused the peoples to the nature of the next War, if it should happen—new and deadly poison gases dropped on cities from the air were then the nightmare of every General Staff—after 1939 we all carried gas-masks for years in Britain.

But Mr. Newton D. Baker was not there to stir Britain and the world to the peril of the Simon statement. The U.S. Delegate was Gibson, Ambassador in Brussels, devoted and admirable, but not trained for parliamentary debate with Simon. Gibson never even tried to move the Conference to a further effort for the Hoover plan; he took Simon's House of Commons statement as Britain's final word.

There were many in the Conference who had come to think of Qualitative Disarmament—of the abolition of forces and weapons of offence—as the system by which Disarmament could be achieved and lasting peace ensured. They were deeply wounded by what seemed to them the British Foreign Secretary's betrayal of the doctrine he had preached. They were to suffer much at Simon's hands in the next 18 months; but his House of Commons Statement of July 7, 1932, was the error they could not forgive.

By that statement Simon killed the Hoover Plan.

And, as events were soon to prove, he killed the Conference, smoothed Adolf Hitler's path to power, and took the nations a long step further towards the Second World War.

CHAPTER 11

The Conference Resolution of July 22nd, 1932

Of course, everybody tried to save something from the wreck.

It was given to the Rapporteur of the General Commission, Edouard Benes, to draw up a Resolution recording the agreements the Conference had achieved, to be adopted by a Plenary Session before the Delegations went home for a summer recess.

This was hard on Benes—he had worked for the Hoover Plan, and had formed a group of eight nations who undertook the task of upholding the rights of the middle and smaller nations against the encroachments of the Great Powers. The group was influential—it included the Delegates of Sweden, Norway, Denmark, the Netherlands, Belgium, Switzerland, Spain and Benes himself (Czechoslovakia).

But Benes had to draft and move the Resolution which the Conference adopted before it adjourned on July 23rd, and his name has remained associated with that gravely inadequate Declaration. During its preparation Simon imposed a veto on the positive statements which Benes and the vast majority of the Conference would have liked to make—on air forces, on bombardment from the air, on tanks, on mobile land guns, on naval armaments.

The section on naval armaments was the least satisfactory of all. It provided that the question should be taken up in "private conversations"—the parties to the Washington and London Treaties were invited to confer and to report to the General Commission.

This section was particularly unwelcome to the middle and smaller nations, who hated "private conversations". But none of the Resolutions really gave them any satisfaction.

The most acceptable phrases were in the preamble, which declared that the Conference was:

"Firmly determined to achieve a first decisive step involving a substantial reduction of armaments, on the basis of Article 8 of the Covenant, and as a natural consequence of the obligations resulting from the Briand–Kellogg Pact, and welcomed heartily the initiative taken by the President of the United States of America in formulating concrete proposals for a substantive reduction of armaments."

The preamble ended by recording the "unanimous decision" of the Conference.

"Guided by the general principles underlying President Hoover's declaration:

i. that a substantial reduction of world armaments shall be effected, to be applied by a General Convention to land, naval and air armaments;

ii. that a primary objective shall be to reduce the means of attack."

The fact that Simons was obliged to accept these words shows how far President Hoover's proposals still dominated the thinking, and embodied the hopes, of the vast majority of the Delegations. But as he still stubbornly adhered to all his own objections which had defeated the Hoover Plan, the High-sounding phrases of the preamble were empty words and nothing more.

So the Delegates thought when they came to discuss and to vote on the Resolution on July 22nd and 23rd. They voted on each paragraph—on one paragraph a Russian amendment was only defeated by 30 votes to 5, with 16 abstentions.

In the end, the large majority of the Delegates who accepted the Resolution as a whole made it plain that they regarded it as quite inadequate.

The President, Arthur Henderson, did the same. He spoke of the great flow of communications from the public and from important NGOs which he had received, assuring him of support for Simon's first Resolution of Qualitative Disarmament, and for "the complete abolition" of aggressive weapons; he said that there had been strong support for equality for Germany; and that he had received "nothing short of a flood of communications in support of the Hoover Plan".

In view of all this powerful expression of public opinion, he found the Resolution "very far short of what I should have liked it to be".

Litvinoff was even more outspoken. Having unsuccessfully proposed amendments which reproduced the detailed concrete proposals of the Hoover Plan, he voted "for Disarmament, and against the Resolution".

Gibson accepted the Resolution with great reluctance, declaring that something much bolder and more decisive should have been done; and he reserved this right to make such proposals in later stages of the Conference.

Italy abstained. It was no longer Grandi who spoke for Italy; he had resigned as Foreign Minister on July 20th. His promising career was over; like the Hoover Plan, it was a casualty of the Simon speech of July 8th. His place was taken by General Balbo, who had earned an unsavoury reputation as Mussolini's Ministers of Air; the Conference found him singularly unsympathetic. Grandi later became Ambassador to London; his fall from ministerial office was a grave blow to the cause of Disarmament and the League.

Finally, Nadolny voted for Germany against the Resolution, and made it plain that no German Delegate would be returning to the Conference, until his nation's full equality of rights in respect of national defence had been formally accepted by all concerned.

Then the Conference adjourned, with the promise that it would meet again on October 1st.

CHAPTER 12

The Disarmament Conference: Autumn, 1932 to Summer 1933

I will only briefly sketch the rest of the history of the Disarmament Conference of 1932–3. Henderson, Boncour, Benes and others were still stubbornly resolved that it must not fail. It became increasingly clear that if there was no Treaty of World Disarmament, Germany would re-arm; and all too soon we knew that, when that happened, Hitler would be man in charge. So certainly it was right to go on trying for a Disarmament Treaty.

But after the defeat of the Hoover Plan, I was obsessed by a growing fear of defeat. The whole proceedings in the Conference seemed to me an anti-climax. I had a conviction that if the "National" Government's hawks could kill the Hoover Plan and still remain in office, they would be able to do the same to any other plan that anyone else could produce.

This craven instinct proved to be right, and I passed a most unhappy year before I finally left Henderson and the Conference in July, 1933.

But before then there had been two other proposals, both of which might have succeeded, and perhaps would have succeeded, but for the continued obstruction and sabotage by hawks, British, French and German.

* * * * *

The first was a proposal by Paul Boncour of France.

When Simon sent Eden then his Parliamentary Under-Secretary as first British delegate to the Conference, Boncour did not follow suit. In September and October, 1932, he was Foreign Minister under Herriot. He continued to attend every meeting of the Conference, and of its Bureau. He was a passionate believer in Disarmament; he had been

Minister of Defence for years, and understood extremely well both the technical problems to be solved in a Disarmament Treaty and the grave military threat France would face if the Conference failed.

During September and October, 1932, he persuaded his Government to accept very drastic proposals for armament reduction, on condition that the perennial "Security" problem could be solved. And when in November he became Prime Minister for 3 weeks, he used his fleeting authority to put forward a comprehensive proposal on which he thought general agreement could be reached. He rightly regarded the Conference as much the most important question with which a French Prime Minister could be engaged.

His Disarmament proposals included the reduction of the numbers of the French Army to equality with those to be allowed to Germany; the reduction of the period of compulsory military service to 6 months, this period to include the days of refresher courses given to "trained reserves" after their compulsory service was over; the abolition of tanks, heavy mobile guns and poison gases; the abolition of national air forces, and the acceptance of Hoover's proposals for the reduction of navies.

So far, this was complete equality with Germany. But France was to be allowed to keep an additional force of land troops to police her colonies. This was not expected to cause much difficulty.

The proposal for the reduction of the period of service to 6 months was an application to manpower of the principle of Qualitative Disarmament. The General Staff Officers at the Conference were all agreed that troops who had received only 6 months' training would be of value for *defensive* operations, but could play no useful part in *offensive* operations.

To meet the demand of his compatriots for Security, Paul-Boncour, of course, wanted the military guarantee of British support, if France, after she had disarmed, should be attacked. But when Simon had assured him that this was impossible—Simon never even thought of challenging Hankey's doctrine of "no further military commitment"—Boncour only asked one thing of Britain; if a nation signatory to the Disarmament Treaty were reported by League Inspectors to be guilty of violating its disarmament obligations, then Britain should join in economic sanctions against the guilty nation. Even this Simon refused.

The rest of Boncour's Security proposal was singularly like Cecil's T.M.A. (Treaty of Mutual Assistance) of 1922–3. He suggested Regional Pacts for Collective Action against aggressors, the nations of each continent to join together against an aggressor.

The British War Office representative in Geneva, Major General A.C. Temperley, who served in all the League Commissions on Armaments for more than 10 years, and who in that time became an ardent and exceptionally able supporter of Disarmament, expressed warm admiration of Paul-Boncour's generous concessions to the Germans.[1]

But Simon cared nothing for that, and nothing for Boncour's efforts to meet British reluctance on security. Of course, the United States and Russia were unwilling to join in Boncour's Continental Pacts, and the countries of the Commonwealth were reluctant too. Simon helped them to sweep into oblivion the proposal on which Boncour had spent long months of effort and on which he had staked his Prime Ministerial reputation. There were discussions about it in the Conference Bureau and some days of debate in the Conference itself, but before Christmas, 1932, it had disappeared from the agenda, and it was never heard of again.

The story of its failure prompts one more reflection on Hankey's doctrine of "No new military commitments".

This doctrine, as put to successive Cabinets by Hankey and other hawks, was in appearance simple, and it convinced many Ministers in office between 1919 and 1939. Britain, said Hankey, has Imperial duties and responsibilities all round the world. She is committed to defend any of the self-governing members of the Commonwealth, or any of her scores of colonies in all the continents, if any of them should ever be attacked. Not only so. She must also maintain bases in every continent for the Royal Navy, and Land Forces in almost every colony to maintain internal order. To meet such heavy commitments, her armed forces were the absolute minimum required—in fact, so argued Hankey, Vansittart and their sympathizers, these forces were always "overstretched". Hankey and Vansittart never lost an opportunity of urging that the forces—all the forces—must be much increased.

Moreover, "whatever we do, war will come", meaning war like that against Germany in 1914, against some foe challenging, as Germany

1 See page 127 below.

was, for "possession" of our Empire, and with only such allies as a Balance of Power policy could produce.

Looking at this strategical position in a realistic way, it was obvious, said Hankey, that Britain could not accept the vague, but perhaps very onerous, additional "commitment" of Article 16—a pledge to fight, not in "our wars", but in someone else's, and with the almost certain result that, once we were involved in dangerous hostilities, the other Members of the League would fail to do their duty, and Britain would be left "carrying the can" against some powerful aggressor, and with the risk of disastrous defeat.

The whole case rested on the twin arguments, constantly repeated by ill-informed Ministers; "Nobody knows what Article 16 means", and "League collective security is a sham, because the foreigners will never fulfill their obligations."

There was no ground for either proposition.

As Sir Cecil Hurst repeatedly explained, Article 16 was crystal clear, and it created a system of mutual guarantees which Britain, if it had been loyal to its legal pledges, could have made extremely, not to say overwhelmingly, strong.

There was very strong support for the League among the great majority of its members. Switzerland, in accepting membership, had been allowed by the other members to make a reservation about its neutrality. This highlighted the fact that the other neutrals of the First World War—the Scandinavians, Holland, Belgium, Spain, the Latin Americans—had made no such reservation.

When the Corfu dispute was at its height with Fascist Italy in 1923, Benes and the Little Entente had made it known that their very powerful armed forces (in fact, stronger than Italy's) would be at the disposal of the League if military sanctions were required to defeat the Duce's Covenant-breaking aggression against Greece. From 1919 onwards, it lay in Britain's power to make the collective security of the League so powerful a reality that neither Mussolini nor anyone else would have dared to risk a Covenant-breaking war. If, under Cecil's T.M.A., or under the Geneva Protocol of 1924, or under the Boncour plan of November, 1932, Britain had pledged her full power against aggression, the era of "national" wars would have ended, and World

Disarmament—the purpose of all these three proposals would have been achieved.

But Hankey and his school were against Disarmament; therefore, they scoffed at, and defeated, all proposals for collective security; and thus they left Britain in 1939 to face the challenge of the Nazis with no Allies but a defeated Poland and a divided France. Simon, in helping to destroy the Boncour plan, paved the way for this terrible 1939 result.

*   *   *

Beyond all expectation, there was one more chance when the Disarmament Conference might have reached agreement. I did not myself in 1933 rate this chance as very high, and I am still more than doubtful whether it would have reached success; but Major General Temperley, whose knowledge of the Geneva situation, and whose authority on the matter, were both far superior to mine, believed that, if British Ministers had really tried, they could have got a Treaty of Disarmament and so avoided the Second World War.

This last chance resulted from the eruption of a slumbering volcano.

Stanley Baldwin was a strange man, and an unpredictable politician.

He is mostly remembered for his lethargy, and for his failure to force decisions which he knew to be necessary and right. There is a legend that he was totally uninterested in foreign policy, a story goes that he used to say in Cabinet to the minister sitting next to him: "Wake me up when you've finished with foreign affairs."

The story was not borne out by the few scraps of conversations I had with him in the lobbies of the House of Commons. In these conversations he sometimes said things which I regarded as Hankey fallacies. But the conversations also showed that he thought a lot about the international situation and the danger of another war. Certainly in May, 1932, he listened gladly to Hugh Gibson, when Gibson came to London to talk about Hoover's views on armaments; he, (Baldwin) even suggested that it might be better, instead of reducing the number of battleships by a third, as Hoover proposed, to abolish them altogether, and so give Germany equality in that regard.[2]

2   This conversation is recorded in the British Cabinet records, but, as I go to Press, I am without the reference to the exact date.

In June, however, he surrendered tamely to his Cabinet hawks and let them destroy the Hoover Plan. But as the year went on, he became more and more concerned about the Conference, and more and more alarmed at the prospect of another war.

On November 10th, 1932, when the prospect looked extremely bleak, his pent-up anxiety exploded out in a famous speech in the House of Commons—the greatest speech he ever made. It was about what would happen if another war broke out.

One phrase of the speech has been remembered and often quoted: "The bomber will always get through."

"I think it is well for the man in the street . . . . . to realize", said Mr. Baldwin, "that there is no power on earth that can prevent him from being bombed. Whatever people may tell him, the bomber will always get through . . . . . The only defence is in offence, which means that you have to kill more women and children more quickly than the enemy, if you want to save yourselves."

(In 1932 this thought still administered a shock.)

"Fear",

Mr. Baldwin went on, and even now we do well to recall his words, "Fear is a very dangerous thing. It is quite true that it may act as a deterrent in people's minds against war, but it is much more likely to make them want to increase armaments to protect themselves against the terrors that they know may be launched against them. We have to remember that aerial warfare is still in its infancy and its potentialities are incalculable and inconceivable."

He then spoke of the "futile attempts" so far made to deal with the problem, such as "reduction of the size of aeroplanes, prohibition of the bombardment of the civil population, the prohibition of bombing." As this was precisely what his Government had put forward on June 27th in their counter-proposals to the Hoover Plan, his sense of frustration must have been acute to make him say in November that such suggestions "reduced him to despair".

"What would be the only object", he asked, "of reducing the size of aeroplanes? . . . . . Immediately every scientific man in the country would turn to making a high explosive bomb about the size of a walnut and as powerful as a bomb of big dimensions.

"The prohibition of the bombardment of the civil population . . . . . is impracticable so long as any bombing exists at all . . . . . If a man has a potential weapon and is going to be killed, he will use that weapon, whatever it is, and whatever undertaking he has given about it. We remember . . . . . the cry that was raised when civilian towns were first bombed (in the 1914 war). It was not long before we replied. . . . . .

"On the solution of this question hangs . . . . . in my view, our civilization. . . . . .

"I am firmly convinced myself, and have been, for some time, that, if it were possible, the air forces ought all to be abolished . . . . . All Disarmament hangs on the Air."

The closing words of this memorable oration were as follows:

"I do not think we have seen the last great war . . . . . It is really for the young to decide . . . . . The instrument is in their hands . . . . . When the next war comes and when European civilization is wiped out, as it will be, and by no force more than by that force, then don't let them lay the blame on the old men. Let them remember that they principally, they alone, are responsible for the terrors that have fallen on the earth".

When he sat down, the House of Commons remained silent for a full minute, and then broke into cheers from every corner of the Chamber that seemed unending. When at last they ceased, everyone knew that Britain would make one more effort to save the Conference; that Baldwin had disavowed and ridiculed his hawks; and that there was new ground for hope.

The speech made a deep impression throughout the world, and not least in Germany. The hope of Disarmament revived among the great majority of the people who longed for it, and in a General Election in December, Hitler's Nazis lost two million votes. The Germans in the Secretariat of the League all said: "That's the end of Hitler. Let's make the Treaty and we shan't hear of him again."

The British Draft Disarmament Treaty

Baldwin followed up his speech without delay. Instructions were sent to Anthony Eden in Geneva to prepare a British plan, in the form of a Draft Treaty for World Disarmament on which general agreement could be reached. Eden was told to work with Major General Temperley and with Sir Alec Cadogan, who had been the head of the League of Nation's Section of the Foreign Office since Tufton's death in 1923.

This was good news, indeed. Temperley and Cadogan were both exceptionally able men; they were both firm supporters of the League and sound, even ardent, disarmers; both carried weight with their departments, and with the Cabinet, at home.

The three men set about their task with zeal. But first there was Christmas; and then they were obstructed by the hawks who imposed delays. Their Draft Treaty was not ready until March 16th, 1933.

They were, of course, diverted from their task by the lamentable proceedings of the League Council and Assembly over Manchuria, in which Simon so grievously misinterpreted the wishes of the British people, and brought such discredit on himself and on his Government. And, of course, the British Government hawks, though disavowed, not to say denounced, by Baldwin on November 10th, did not give up their opposition. Eyres–Monsell continued to oppose the scrapping of any British warship; Hailsham went on urging that we must keep tanks and heavy mobile guns; Londonderry was immovably in support both of bombers and of bombing.

No doubt all this was known to German militarist spies. No doubt it inspired their leaders to an act of treacherous, but successful, bluff. General von Schleicher had been allowed to become the Chancellor of the Reich. At the end of January he could claim that the British, after the Disarmament Conference had lasted for a year, were still firmly resolved to deny to Germany the equality of rights in national defence to which she was entitled under the Treaty of Versailles. Therefore there would be no Disarmament Treaty to which Germany could agree; the Western Allies had torn up their Treaty obligations, and Germany must be free to take the course which her vital national interests required.

With this specious argument—*specious* in view of Baldwin's speech, of the feeling of the British people, and the general attitude of the Delegations in Geneva, but with too much solid fact to support it—the militarist leaders of the Reich ventured a daring *coup d'etat*.

General von Schleicher, until the General Election of December 1932, like the other militarists, had been calculating that the propaganda of the *Hugenberg Konzern* would inevitably bring Hitler into power, with majority support of the German people. But Hitler's heavy electoral defeat in that month threw this into serious doubt. If the British in the end produced an acceptable disarmament Treaty, Hitler would disappear, and their chance of re-arming Germany would be gone.

So, on January 31st, 1933, von Schleicher persuaded the President of the Weimar Republic, the aged Field Marshal Hindenburg, to name Hitler as Chancellor in succession to himself. Hindenburg had been trusted as an honourable man, and it was confidently said that he was no longer in command of his faculties when he agreed to what von Schleicher proposed. In any case, between them they tore up the Weimar Constitution. Hitler came to power with no mandate from the German people—and he never had one. He held a General Election in March, 1933. Before it took place, he had outlawed the Communist Party and so disenfranchised a sizeable proportion of the electorate; at the polls, the S.A. and S.S. forcibly prevented great numbers of Social Democrats and Liberals from casting their votes. Even so, Hitler was short of a majority in the Reichstag; he only scraped through with the support of 30-odd "Nationalists" led by Hugenberg, who declared that he was not a Nazi, but who, nevertheless was willing to help the Nazis to destroy democracy.

This Hitler proceeded to do with a vengeance. Very shortly he burnt the Reichstag building, as a symbolic forecast of what he meant to do. He faked the trial of a Bulgarian Communist, whom he falsely accused of the Reichstag crime.

It is sometimes said—Vansittart and Dalton used to say it—that the German democrats should have been able to resist these acts of constitution-breaking force. The short answer is that they *did* resist them; hundreds of thousands of them were thrown into concentration camps, and were tortured to death—Buchenwald alone boasted 58,000 victims who perished in agony.

But effective resistance was not only hopeless; it was impossible. Hitler had the backing of the General Staffs and of their long-term volunteer troops, who had been trained in iron discipline. He had the SS and SA Blackshirts; German youth, unemployed and starving, thanks to the world slump, had joined him by the hundred thousand, and they included almost every student in several generations of university graduates. In his first weeks in power, Hitler showed that he meant to re-establish universal military service, and to re-animate the aggressive German militarist spirit by every means in his power.

It was against this gloomy background of events not far away that Eden, Temperley and Cadogan had to do their work.

Their Draft Treaty of World Disarmament was a big improvement on the earlier proposals which Simon circulated to the Conference in Geneva on July 7th, 1932.

Politically, in March, 1933, the chapter on Land Forces was the most important.

Temperley's articles provided that the period of training should be 8 months, including the days of refresher courses for trained forces agreed. It was generally agreed that this would transform the European continental armies into short-service militias, incapable, by lack of training, of conducting the offensive operations of aggressive war.

Temperley also inserted a Table or Schedule showing the actual number of troops to be allowed in its peace-time army to each of the fourteen most important European Powers. This gave 200,000 men in their home country to France, Germany, Italy and Poland; France to be allowed 200,000 more in her colonies overseas; 500,000 to the Soviet; 150,000 to Romania; 120,000 to Spain; 100,000 to Czechoslovakia; 60,000 to Greece; only 25,000 to the Netherlands.

This Table is still of great interest, because Temperley was convinced that it would have been accepted, if the British Government had seriously tried to press it home. His figures were so low that they would have meant a drastic de-militarization of Europe in 1933; in 1978 they look like numbers suitable for a system of general and complete disarmament.

Temperley was not so successful with the offensive weapons.

The British hawks insisted that tanks not exceeding 16 tons in weight must be permitted—Britain had 16 such tanks in 1932 and many fewer than Hitler in 1939. Temperley provided that the number of permitted tanks must be restricted; but he suggested no actual figures, and much, of course, would have depended on that.

On heavy mobile guns, the hawks were victorious again. The

British Draft did not propose the scrapping of *existing* guns, but only a limitation of future replacement guns to 105 mm (4.1-inch) calibre.

Of course, the Draft proposed the total abolition of all chemical weapons, including those which made use of fire.

The naval chapter was total victory for Eyres–Monsell. It proposed that other naval powers not signatory to the Washington and London Naval Treaties should accept reductions and restrictions which would make them, in effect, parties to those Treaties. Britain, the U.S.A. and Japan would make no further reductions in their fleets in 1933, but would consider such reductions in a separate Naval Conference to be held in 1935.

Londonderry was only less victorious than Eyres–Monsell. "All Disarmament turns on the Air", said Baldwin. He had been firmly convinced for some time that, "if it were possible, the air forces ought to be abolished".

"If it were possible" meant "if a sound scheme could be found for ensuring that civil aircraft would not be used in wartime by an aggressor to bombard his victim."

It was this alleged danger, and this alone, that prevented Baldwin from insisting on the total and immediate abolition of all air forces – and if he had so insisted, the British Draft Convention would have had a far greater prospect of success.

In fact, two practicable plans were laid before the Conference for dealing with the danger of civil aviation. On the scale on which it then existed, it constituted no military danger whatever. But the hawks successfully pooh-poohed the Belgian and Swedish plans, and exploited the bogey they had invented.

So the British Draft Convention contained some of the provisions which Baldwin had ridiculed in the House of Commons. Thus:

An unladen weight of 3 tons was taken as the size of aircraft which could not be used for bombing or other offensive operations.

Aircraft of over this weight were to be destroyed within 5 years.

Exceptions were allowed for troop-carrying aircraft and flying boats.

The numbers of aircraft allowed to each Signatory Power were to be drastically reduced from the levels that existed in 1933.

The Great Powers were to be allowed a total of 500 each, supplemented by "an immediate reserve" of 125. This number was to cover all aircraft in land, naval and air forces, and to include the troop carriers and flying boats, if any. Sweden was to be allowed 75, and other nations less.

Bombing from the air was to be abolished by international law, and a provision to this effect was included in the British Draft Convention. It was originally accompanied by a reservation that Britain might continue to bomb the North West frontier of India, but under the pressure of other nations in the Conference, this reservation was dropped.

So far, Baldwin had made fairly large concessions to his hawks. But there was one proposal which, in his opinion, bought back all the rest.

This was the part of the British Draft Convention which provided for the establishment of a Permanent Disarmament Commission, the task of which was not only to supervise and ensure the faithful observance of the obligations undertaken by the Parties, but also to prepare agreements for further steps in Disarmament at future conferences.

The Air Chapter of the British Draft contained the following Article:

"The Permanent Disarmament Commission . . . . . shall immediately devote itself to the working out of the best possible schemes providing for:

(a)   the complete abolition of military and naval aircraft, which must be dependent on the effective supervision of civil aviation to prevent its misuse for military purposes.

(b)   the schemes prepared by the P.D.C. shall be reported to the Second Disarmament Conference." (In 5 years' time.)

This Article was the best hope that the British Draft Convention would be accepted by the Conference. The rest of the air provisions look fairly drastic in 1978, and in 1933 they would have meant something like a 60 per cent reduction of the numbers of military and naval aircraft then possessed by Britain, France and other major Powers; and they would have meant a far greater cut than that in the *offensive* power of the various national forces. They would have prevented the development of the heavy bomber, and would have given time for public opinion to force the acceptance of the measures needed for the total abolition of national air forces, and for the internationalization or international control of civil aviation.

But in March, 1933, these proposals were received with disappointment by the Conference. The Delegations had been expecting something better from Stanley Baldwin; they did not relish at all the proposed 5-year delay in achieving the abolition of military aviation.

And, of course, Hitler's Delegates were swift to point out that the whole British plan was very far from acceptance of the system of Part V of the Treaty of Versailles, by which, they constantly insisted, the other nations were morally, and legally, bound.

To increase the chance that the British Draft Convention would be accepted, Baldwin insisted that the Prime Minister and Foreign Secretary, MacDonald and Simon, should go themselves to Geneva for its presentation to the Conference, and that MacDonald should make the necessary speech.

They arrived on March 8th and, on the afternoon of March 10th, MacDonald laid the plan prepared by Eden, Temperley and Cadogan before a full gathering of Delegates. Herriot had come from Paris to join Boncour; Litvinoff was still there; but there was no Grandi, only an obstructive Baron Aloisi to speak for Italy; and the German Delegates were in a very different frame of mind from that of Herr Nadolny when Hugh Gibson had explained the Hoover Plan 9 months before.

Of course, it should have been a very great occasion. It was, in fact, as events were soon to prove, the last day on which the Conference had a real chance of reaching practical results. But it was very "flat" from first to last.

Principally to blame was the almost catastrophic failure of MacDonald's speech. Simon, with characteristic sycophancy, reported to the Cabinet that the Prime Minister had been "in his finest form", and that he had made a "deep impression on the Delegates."

But, by chance, I was not sitting on Arthur Henderson's presidential dais while MacDonald was speaking; instead, I suppose at her invitation, I was sitting in the public gallery next to MacDonald's daughter, Ishbel. When MacDonald sat down, amid rather perfunctory applause, Ishbel's righthand neighbour turned to her and said: "That was a very fine speech." "Oh no", answered Ishbel, "My father was not at all in his best form", and she was in very evident distress that this should have been so.

In fact, it was painfully evident throughout the speech that Mac-Donald's powers, under the stress of many years of over-work, of too little sleep, of grave responsibility, had begun to fail. It seemed to me that he had great difficulty in bringing his sentences to a grammatical conclusion, and that he did not always succeed. His voice sounded quite unlike his usual fluent and resonant delivery. He made the grave mistake of "talking down" to his non-British audience.

But Temperley was convinced that all was not yet lost. *His* proposals for the drastic reduction of the European continental armies had, indeed, made a deep impression; and they went far to giving Germany real equality in the armaments that mattered most to France and her allies.

Years afterwards, in 1938, with the shadow of the Second World War hanging over him, Temperley wrote in his invaluable book, *The Whispering Gallery of Europe*, his explanation of why the British Draft had failed, when, in his belief it could have been made to succeed.

He had expected that his table of figures, proposing the permitted strengths of the European armies, would be received with widespread opposition and perhaps resentment. He records that, in fact,

"the figures were well received. Several of the Delegates came to see me, and asked for increases of their own, but there was almost an entire absence of general criticism."

He believed that with bold leadership at the highest level (i.e. from the Prime Minister and Foreign Secretary), the Conference could have been persuaded to accept the Draft Convention as a whole.

"It is a deep conviction of mine", he wrote in 1938, "that it would have succeeded, and as time brings an added perspective, the more certain am I that I am right. I was in close touch with the general feeling of the time and I am sure that there was very grave anxiety about the fate of the Conference and the gathering storms. The immense advance by the French towards the German point of view was a most favourable sign, although it proved to be too late . . . . . We should have been sure of American and Italian backing, and the French and Germans could have hardly said 'No' . . . . . The chance was lost because it was never realized by those at home what a winner we had in our stable."[3]

3   Major General A. C. Temperley, *The Whispering Gallery of Europe*, pp. 235–6, 243, 244.

Everyone must accept the high authority and high sincerity of these words.

But many of "those at home" were not concerned at all about "having a winner" in our Geneva stable. They were thinking of other things. Vansittart and Hankey were engaged in their long (and futile) campaign to bring about an alliance with Mussolini's Italy against Hitler's Germany. And on March 17th, 1933, Vansittart had one of his most startling successes—a success that was fatal to Temperley's hopes.

The gloomy non-success of MacDonald's Conference speech on March 16th had been a serious setback to those hopes. A heartwarming oratorical success, such as MacDonald could have achieved if he had been in his best form, would have transformed the Conference atmosphere, and filled the Delegations with a new and ardent belief in their mission to de-militarize the world and abolish war. MacDonald's speech had not done this; on the contrary, it had dispirited the keen disarmers in the Conference, and concentrated their attention on the shortcomings of the plan which he proposed.

But worse was to come on the following day. So, far from staying in Geneva and giving bold leadership at the highest level in support of the British Draft Convention, MacDonald and Simon incontinently took a train on the very next morning, and went to—Rome!

They did not even go to seek the Italian support for their Draft Convention which Temperley was sure they could have had.

They went on a very different mission. Vansittart had been encouraging Mussolini to press a plan which the Duce had conceived for the creation of a new European Council to consist of the Four Great Powers. Britain, France, Germany and Italy—Germany meaning Hitler, and Italy, Mussolini.

This Council, as the Duce planned, would replace the Council of the League in all important European matters—it would, of course, be attended by the most senior ministers, while the League could be left to diplomats or other juniors.

This sinister conspiracy ended in fiasco, because the pro-League forces in Europe were too strong. Cecil, of course, exposed and denounced it. Cecil's close personal friend, Cosmo Lang, the Archibishop of Canterbury, preached a famous sermon in his cathedral, which was broadcast to the Commonwealth, in which he described as "germs of infection" those who sought to undermine the authority of the League; Liberal, Labour and considerable Conservative opinion was mobilized. The Duce's plan was killed.

But it had served one purpose. No doubt it was not by accident that MacDonald and Simon left Geneva within hours of the time when they unveiled the British Draft Disarmament Convention. It was not by accident that they had gone to Rome, to discuss with the Fascist dictator his disloyal machinations against the League.

All this had been carefully planned, times and dates and trains, by Vansittart as a vital step in his campaign.

And no doubt Vansittart had beseeched the Duce to take special trouble with the failing British Prime Minister. In any case, Mussolini achieved an almost fabulous success. In his report to the Cabinet after his return from Rome, MacDonald spoke in glowing terms of the intellectual power and the charm of the Duce; he praised the marvellous efficiency of the Fascist administration and of the economy of Italy; he even went so far as to say that the Fascists had achieved a widespread and remarkable "spiritual development"[4] of the Italian people.

It was an astonishing result of Vansittart's sustained campaign of propaganda that MacDonald could address such language to his Cabinet colleagues. Only a few years later the Second World War was to show that the Italian people were far gone in political division and social corruption, Fascism was to disappear, and Mussolini to perish, in a welter of ignominious defeat. MacDonald's judgements of 1933 were as wrong-headed and as superficial as Vansittart's propaganda. But MacDonald's judgements were worse than wrong-headed and superficial. He was a life-long Social Democrat; that he should speak of a "spiritual revival of the Italian peoople" achieved by cudgels, castor-oil and killing is hard to forgive, even after 40 years. The blood of Matteotte, the greatest Socialist, the greatest Italian, and perhaps the greatest European, of his time, should have served to clear MacDonald's vision of the synthetic falsehoods by which it was obscured.

But so far as the British Draft Convention was concerned, Vansittart's plot had worked. I remember very clearly the dismay with which the British delegation and the British journalists learnt that the two ministers had disappeared, and that they had gone to Rome. I remember

4   Quoted by George Scott, *The Rise and Fall of the League of Nations*, p. 277.

just as clearly the disillusioned comments of the foreign Delegates; they naturally concluded that the British Government could not greatly care about their Draft Convention, if MacDonald's speech was the sum of the top-level support that it would get.

But many people in the Conference still tried very hard to make the British Plan succeed.

Simon came back from time to time to play a part. In between his visits, Eden carried on, always acting strictly in accordance with the instructions which he received from the hawks at home.

The U.S. Delegation behaved with great generosity and zeal. They often said they still liked Hoover's Plan better than the British Plan. They still tried to persuade the British to give up their fixed obsession about tanks and battleships and military aircraft. But they gave their loyal support to the British and to the Conference. In the summer of 1933 there were suspensions of the Conference for "private talks" among the Powers, and demands by Benes' group of 8 that the Conference sittings must be resumed. But neither private talks nor open debate brought the British along the road to the system of the Treaty of Versailles.

In the end, Franklin Roosevelt who had replaced Herbert Hoover as President, instructed Norman Davies to say that the United States would accept the full application to its armed forces of every provision in Part V of the Treaty of Versailles, if this would induce all other governments to do the same.[5]

President Roosevelt had written a few weeks before: "If all nations will agree whooly to eliminate from possession and use weapons which make possible a successful attack, defence automatically will become impregnable, and the frontiers and independence of every nation will become secure".[6]

His Part V offer was a remarkable, and courageous act of statesmanship. If the British and French Governments had foreseen the future as clearly as Henderson and Cecil foresaw it, they would have leapt at Roosevelt's offer, and made it the basis of the World Treaty they all desired.

5   Minutes of the General Commission of the Disarmament Conference, May, 1933, pp. 461–2.
6   *11A Survey 1933, pp. 27–3.*

For Germany was already being re-armed, and re-armed by Hitler. It was clear that the German forces would be stronger than any nation had ever been before; that Hitler would not hesitate to put his concept of "total war" into remorseless application in aggression against one or both of them.

If they had then quickly got a Treaty on the Versailles basis, both Russia and the United States would have signed it. Germany would have still been bound by the restrictions she had accepted in 1919. In this case she would have been literally unable to commit aggression against France or Britain—she would not have had the forces or the offensive arms to do it.

There would have been on-site inspection of the observance of the Treaty by international teams of League inspectors. If Hitler or Mussolini had tried to cheat, and to increase their armaments above the level which the Treaty allowed, they would inevitably have been discovered at an early stage. When discovered and reported to the League, the anger of the whole world would have been mobilized against them, and there would have been an excellent chance that world opinion, with the British people leading, would have insisted that the economic sanctions of Article 16 should be applied, and that this would have ended the aggressive dictator's term of power.

This is not simply a retrospective fantasy of mine. When he lamentably died at an early age, there was general agreement that Captain Basil Liddell Hart was the most learned, the most penetrating and the wisest authority on the study of modern war. Writing in 1961, Liddell Hart said that if the Hoover Plan had been accepted, "as it nearly was", and if tanks and bombers had been abolished, as they would have been, then the Axis aggressions of 1939–40 would have been "impossible". And he argued at length that they could *not* have cheated, because tanks and bombers could not be built in secret—the League inspectors would certainly have found it out; and if, by a miracle, they *had* been built in secret, that would not have permitted the aggressions to take place, for tanks and bombers are useless unless their crews have been long and carefully trained in constant exercises, which would have advertised the aggressors' disloyal intentions to the whole world.[7]

Thus Liddell Hart's high authority condemns the strategic mad-

7 Liddel Hart, *Defence or Deterrence*, 1961, pp. 256–7.

ness of the British hawks, Douglas Hogg and Londonderry, who insisted on retaining tanks and bombers. The case against Eyres–Monsell is just as strong. If Britain had accepted the abolition, by Hoover's stages, of battleships and aircraft carriers, then submarines would have been abolished, too. And in the war of 1939, the British battleships played a negligible part in our national defence; our aircraft carriers were vulnerable in a very high degree to submarine and bomber attack; but Hitler's submarines nearly brought the British Empire to its knees.

It need not be argued further that Britain and France made a disastrous error when they turned down Franklin Roosevelt's offer to accept the world-wide application of the system of Part V of the Treaty of Versailles. In 1932 General Georges, the ablest of Paul-Boncour's military advisers, had said: "Inspection is security." That was a bold statement in 1932 by a member of the French General Staff.

If Britain and France had accepted Roosevelt's offer, they might have discovered that *Disarmament* is security—a proposition which should be as incontrovertible in 1978, as it would have been in 1933 or 1939.

By rejecting Roosevelt's proposition, by insisting on retention of their "offensive weapons", their tanks and bombers and heavy mobile guns and battleships, they ensured their defeat by Hitler, the occupation and slavery of France, the inglorious, though glorious retreats from Dunkirk and Greece and Crete.

Their refusal of Roosevelt's offer sealed the fate of the Geneva Conference. There were still brave efforts to use the British Draft Convention as the basis of the World Treaty that nearly everyone desired. The pressure of the Conference induced the British, as said above, to give up their reservation about bombing on the North West Frontier. At an even later stage, they agreed to the abolition of all tanks.

But this was all too late. The German Delegation became more and more difficult to please—not to say obstructive. The Conference debates were interrupted in order that the Great Powers might persuade them in private talks. The private talks demoralized the other Delegations, but, apart from that, led to no result—it was far easier for hawks to sabotage in private than when the press were looking on.

And always there were doubts whether the British, meaning two-faced Simon, really *wanted* a result. Certainly some of his Cabinet colleagues, still resisting Baldwin, did *not*.

So, after many ups and downs, and much loyal work by the United States, Davies and Gibson, the Conference decided once more on a July adjournment. They agreed to meet again in October, 1933, and that then they would begin what they called a "Second Reading" debate on the British Draft. In the meantime the Bureau of the Conference was to do some work, and the Great Powers were to seek agreement in private talks.

I felt so little confidence in these decisions that I decided to leave Henderson and go home to London to resume my private work. I had had the happiest relations with Henderson, and in July, 1933, my admiration and affection for him were as undimmed as they still remain today.

But I felt small regret in 1933, and I feel none at all today. My "private work" was helping the League of Nations Union to plan, prepare and organize the "Peace Ballot" of 1934–5; and to make progress with my book, *The Private Manufacture of Armaments*, which was published in 1936.

Nothing that happened in Geneva caused me to think that my decision to leave Henderson had been wrong.

During the summer adjournment of 1933, the Bureau of the Conference did nothing that was worthwhile. The private talks among the Powers led to nothing at all. On October 14 Hitler's Germany announced that it had left the Conference and would not return. A few days later it announced that it had left the League.

The hawks had won. The Conference was dead. The vibrant hopes inspired by the Hoover Plan became a mocking memory. It was more than two decades before Kruschev, with genius, courage and imagination, endeavoured to revive them. In 1933 the Governments turned their backs on Disarmament, and were soon engaged in the fiercest arms race which, up to then, the world had ever known.

In the League Assembly in September, 1933, Simon made a speech in which he said that the Conference had solved all the "technical" problems of Disarmament; that nothing was needed but the "political will" to make the Treaty and to carry it out.

The political will had existed in ample measure among all the peoples of the world, and among many of the Governments. The hawks had only won a narrow victory. If Major General Temperley was right, it was very narrow indeed.

CHAPTER 13

The Great Betrayal by the Hawks

When the British hawks, with the help of French and German sympathizers, compelled the luckless Simon to kill the Hoover Plan, they betrayed the vital military interest of the British people.

Eyres–Monsell, egged on by Hankey and Vansittart, insisted that Britain must retain her battleships and aircraft carriers, although this meant that submarines would remain as well.

Douglas Hogg insisted that we must keep 6-inch mobile guns and tanks. Lord Londonderry insisted that we must keep the bombers.

Strategic Madness

They destroyed the Conference, and launched the nations on the deadliest arms race the world had ever known.

Three years after the failure of Stanley Baldwin's Draft Disarmament Convention, Sir Winston Churchill said in the House of Commons:

"I cannot believe that after armaments of all countries have reached a towering height, they will settle down and continue at a hideous level, far above the present level, already crushing—and that that will be for many years a normal feature of the world routine.

"Whatever happens, I do not believe that. Europe is approaching a climax. I believe that climax will be reached during the lifetime of the present Parliament. Either there will be a melting of hearts and a joining of hands between great nations—which will set out to realise the glorious age of prosperity now within the reach of millions of toiling people—or there will be an explosion and a catastrophe, the course of which no human eye can see'.[1]

1 *Hansard*, April 23rd, 1936, Col. 339.

If Winston Churchill were alive in 1978, he would repeat that warning. The level of armaments are higher than in 1936, or indeed in 1939; and the weapons are more dangerous.

Three years after he spoke the words which I have quoted, the Second World War began.

Within a few months, the stand of the British militarists against the Hoover Plan was proved to be strategic madness.

They had "saved" the bomber and the tank; and it was with tanks and bombers that Hitler conquered Europe.

They had saved the battleship, and with the battleship, they saved the submarine. And Hitler's submarines came near to bringing the British Empire to its knees.

When the War was long since over, in 1961, Captain Basil Liddell Hart, the most respected of military historians, wrote as follows:

"If tanks and bomber-aircraft had been universally abolished in 1932 as was then proposed—*and nearly agreed*—and a system of international inspection established as a check on their revival, there could have been no successful *Blitzkrieg* in 1939–40. For Hitler owed his initial victories mainly to those particular defence-breaking weapons. Numbers of troops counted for little in comparison. Indeed, his opponents had the superiority in that respect."[2]

Liddell Hart went on to argue that, if tanks and bombers had been abolished, Hitler and Mussolini would not have found it possible to cheat—those weapons could not be manufactured in secret, nor tested in secret, nor could their crews have been trained in secret. And:

"Tanks and Bombers", he said, "largely depend for their effectiveness on their crews having operational practice in exercises—and such practice could hardly have been hidden".[3]

No blitzkrieg? No War.

Political Betrayal

The British hawks in 1932 betrayed the ardent will of the British people that the nations of the world should mutually disarm.

Two major political events prove beyond all doubt that that is true

On October 25th, 1933, 3 months after the Delegations to the

2   B. H. Liddel Hart, *Deterrent or Defence* p. 250. My italics.
3   *loc. cit.,* p. 251.

Disarmament Conference had left Geneva for the last time, there was a Bye-Election in the London Borough of Fulham (East).

In the General Election held exactly 2 years before, a supporter of the National Government had been returned to Parliament by the following vote:

Lt. Col. Sir K. P. Vaughan Morgan ("National")	23,438
Sir John Maynard (Labour)	8,917
J. H. Greenwood (Liberal)	1,788

Thus the majority of the "National" Government candidate in October, 1931, was *14,521*; he received almost *three* times as many votes as his Labour opponent.

In the Bye-Election in October 1933, the Labour candidate, Mr. John Wilmot, conducted his whole campaign, from the first day to the last, on Disarmament Conference, on Sir John Simon's disastrous opposition to the Hoover Plan, and on the National Government's guilt for the fact that the Conference had failed.

Mr. Wilmot hardly spoke of any other issue; he brought every meeting, every Press Conference, every confrontation with opponents or friends, back to the crucial issue of Disarmament, and what the disaster in Geneva would mean to the British people and to the world.

The result of the Election on October 25th was as follows:

John Wilmot (Labour)	17,790
W. J. Waldren ("National")	12,950
Labour majority	4,840

Mr. Wilmot had almost exactly doubled the Labour vote; the "National" candidate had lost almost half the votes his predecessor had received 2 years before.

The swing away from the "National" Government was the largest anyone could remember in any Bye-Election for many years.

Mr. Wilmot told the House of Commons that his victory was "the result of a passionate and insistant demand for peace, but a demand that that desire should be translated with some practical disarmament accomplishment."[4]

No one in the British Press ventured to dispute his verdict.

4 *Hansard,* Nov 13, 1933.

The "Peace Ballot", 1934-5

The Peace Ballot was carried out by the joint action of 39 British non-governmental organizations under the leadership of Lord Cecil.

The campaign was undertaken in answer to a campaign by hawks who urged that Britain should leave the League of Nations, that Britain should declare that she would attend no more Disarmament Conferences, and demanded (as Vansittart did) that the Government should rapidly build up the strength of our armed forces, and particularly of the Royal Air Force.

The Peace Ballot campaign lasted 9 months, from October 1934 to July 1935. Its purpose was to ask the electors of Britain to answer 6 questions about the League of Nations, World Disarmament, and the prevention of aggressive war.

But it was not a mere opinion poll. There was an intense, sustained effort of public education about the issues which the 6 questions involved.

The National Ballot Committee prepared a large quantity of high-grade literature, in which the arguments for and against the League and World Disarmament were fully and authoritatively discussed.

There were thousands of public meetings, with speakers of national standing, packed audiences and lively question times.

There was a daily flood of news about the Ballot and its progress in the Press.

Editors printed letters on the subject by the score—editors of both the national and local papers.

Some papers—a very few—stirred up public interest by opposing the Ballot, and denouncing Cecil and others who had got it up.

The *Daily Express,* with its enormous circulation, helped a lot by calling the enterprise "The Ballot of Blood". (The hawk line at this time was increasingly to say that anyone who backed the League was in favour of war—"War monger" was shouted almost daily across the House of Commons by the militarists there.

In every Parliamentary constituency—more than 600 of them—a Ballot Committee was set up, with leading citizens of all Parties, and leading clergymen and non-Party people taking part.

More than £100,000—in those days a lot of money—was collected in shilings and half-crowns to finance the work.

More than *half a million* canvassers volunteered to distribute the Ballot papers with the 6 questions to every family in every house in town and country throughout the whole of Britain. The canvassers gave explanatory literature to the electors, if the electors asked for it; they explained the questions, and answered difficulties or objections which might be raised. After a proper interval, they collected the Ballot papers with the answers given, sometimes calling 6 or 7 times at a house where the answers were slow to come.

This educational campaign was more thorough, and sustained for a much longer time, than any Party political campaign in a General Election.

When the day arrived for the collection and counting of the votes in each town or district, an impartial committee of leading citizens was established to do the count.

When the whole operation was completed, the final national result was declared by Cecil at a meeting in the Albert Hall in London, with the Archbishop of Canterbury in the Chair.

The figures amazed even the most optimistic of those who had organized the Ballot:

National Result of the Peace Ballot

Questions	Answers Yes	Answers No	Total Vote	% of total vote who answered Yes*
Question 1: Should Great Britain remain a Member of the League of Nations?				
	10,642,500	337,064	11,087,660	*97.0
Question 2: Are you in favour of an all-round reduction of armaments by international agreement?				
	10,058,526	815,565	11,087,660	*92.5
Question 3: Are you in favour of the all-round abolition of national military and naval aircraft by international agreement?				
	9,157,145	1,614,159	11,087,660	*85.0

Questions	Answers Yes	Answers No	Total Vote	% of total vote who answered Yes*
Question 4: Should the manufacture and sale of armaments for private profit be prohibited by international agreement?				
	10,002,849	740,354	11,087,660	*93.1
Question 5: Do you consider that, if a nation insists on attacking another, the other nations should combine to compel it to stop by				
(a) economic and non-military measures?				
	9,627,606	740,354		94.1
(b) if necessary, military measures?				
	8,506,777	2,262,261		74.2

*The disparity between the total answers sent in and the total of the Yes and No answers is explained by the fact that the full Table of Results showed some "Doubtfuls" and some "Abstentions on each question. Only on 5 (B) were the numbers significant, so I have omitted them here.

Every organ of the Press agreed that these results were a triumph for Cecil and the policies for which he stood.

When they began to organize the Ballot, he and his colleagues had agreed that, if they could get 4 million answers, that would be a great success; and the vote, whatever it might be, would reflect the true opinion of the British people on the League, Disarmament, and the prevention of aggressive War.

In the event, they got more than 11 million answers, almost 3 times as many as they had dared to hope for.

The votes cast in favour of the League and World Disarmament were more than the largest number that had ever put a Party Political Government in power.

The vote on Question 3 showed that the British people were over-whelmingly in favour of abolishing warfare in the air.

As the results came in from different towns and districts over the 9 months of the campaign, Mussolini's preparation for his Abyssinian war were going forward. As the war came nearer, the majority for sanctions progressively increased. In the end, the majority for economic sanctions was the second highest—94.1 per cent, near unanimity of the British people.

There was more hesitation about military sanctions if they should be required. More than 2 million people abstained from voting; they had not made up their minds.

But the vote for stopping Mussolini, by armed force if that should be required, was 74.2 per cent, three to one in favour, and no one doubted that this represented the true feeling of the British people.

The Peace Ballot proved beyond a doubt that the British people understood the policy of World Disarmament and the collective security of the League. It proved that Hankey and the hawks had betrayed the wishes of the British people when they destroyed Cecil's Treaty of Mutual Assistance, the Geneva Protocol, the Coolidge Conference, and the Disarmament Conference of 1932. It proved that the British people wanted to fulfill the legal obligations of the Covenant which they had signed.

In 1939 to 1945 the British people paid a heavy price for the errors and betrayals of the hawks. For, as Churchill said, in words already quoted in other chapters above, the Second World War could *"easily"* have been prevented, if their will to uphold the League of Nations had been permitted to prevail!

CHAPTER 14

Conclusion

Let the reader turn back a few pages and look again at what Sir Winston Churchill said in the House of Commons in April, 1936.

It is, perhaps, the most powerful statement of the dangers of the arms race ever made; only Czar Nicholas II's Rescript of 1898 can bear comparison.

Let the reader consider how similar is the international situation of 1978 to that of 1936—the same desperate expenditure of resources on the building up of armies, navies and air forces, and on accumulating stocks of arms; the same confusion in the international exchanges; the same stagnation of international trade; the same distorted propaganda by both the rival camps; the same anxiety about impending war.

Let the reader learn from earlier pages that World Disarmament can only be achieved by statesmen at the highest level of political responsibility; that underlings will never obtan any significant result; that Prime Ministers and Foreign Secretaries and Ministers of Defence have no other work of comparable importance; that they should make it, as Professor Isida Rabi[1] said in 1956, their top priority every day; that there is no technical problem in making a Treaty of General and Complete Disarmament that has not already been solved;

but that the Heads of Governments must steel themselves for a long and bitter battle with the hawks, if they are to win;

and that everything must be done in public, it is in secret that the hawks can exercise their power.

Let the reader remember that for every man and woman in the world, and for every child, the issue of World Disarmament and World Development is incomparably the most important question he will ever

1   Prof. Isida Rabi was an A-bomb expert, and Chairman of President Eisenhower's Advisory Committee of Scientists.

face; that he must choose, as Mr. Gordon Dean said in 1956, "between Peace and Oblivion"; that the choice must be made, not in some distant future, but in the coming months and years; and that each man's and woman's voice and vote can help to make it "Peace."[2]

Last, let the reader remember that it was President Eisenhower, the victorious Commander of the greatest forces in the greatest battle in history, who said that: "War in our time has become an anachronism. Whatever the case in the past, war in the future can serve no useful purpose".[3]

If War is an anachronism, so are the armaments with which wars are fought.

When scientists and engineers destroyed the barriers of time and space between the nations, they ushered out the old epoch of power politics and recurrent conflict, and ushered in the new epoch in which all nations must cooperate to use their common flow of wealth for the promotion of their common good.

2   Gordon Dean was the first Chairman of the U.S. Atomic Energy Commission who built up large stocks of nuclear weapons, but who was dismissed from his office because he asked the question "when is enough enough?" By the word "Oblivion" Mr. Dean meant the extermination of the human race. He proposed a world-wide educational campaign by every organ of every Government to make the people understand the mortal peril of modern armaments and modern war.
3   Address to U.S. Society of Newspaper Editors, April 21st, 1956.

By the same Author

The Geneva Protocol (1925)

Disarmament (1926)

The Coolidge Conference (1927)

The Juridical Status of the British
   Dominions in International Law (1929)

The Private Manufacture of Armaments (1936 and 1972)

The Arms Race (1958 and 1960)

Index